MW01026626

A Work of Lace

Silence Speaks

By

Betty Smyth Vaden

A Work of Lace
Silence Speaks

Copyright © 2021 by Betty Smyth Vaden. All rights reserved. No part of this book may be reproduced, stored in a retrieval system or transmitted in any way by any means, whether electronic, mechanical, photocopy, or recording unless prior written permission is obtained from the author.

Scripture quotations marked NLT are taken from the *Holy Bible, New Living Translation copyright © 1996, 2004, 2007 and are used according to their guidelines.*

Scripture quotations marked KJV are taken from the *Holy Bible, The King James Version. Public Domain.*

To My Children

Children, you are the most valuable gifts ever bestowed unto me, and my prayer is that you rest in God's everlasting love. I pray that He will soften your scars of life and empower you to soar into His presence where you will transcend the frailty of this pilgrim journey and lay hold of His perfect peace. May the heavenly Father grant you the understanding to learn from my tattered lace, and to look forward because you have an inheritance awaiting you that is undefiled. This assembly of words is dedicated to you, beloved children, my blessing and my heart in this earthly walk.

Contents

Acknowledgments

Most significantly, I bow before You, dear Father, for urging me to unveil my defeats and victories to all who need hope. You have taken me from the ash heap and planted me by waters as a beautiful and mighty oak to display Your righteousness and splendor. May all praise be extolled to You for truth expounded in this written effort. When I have been weak, You have been strong. When I have failed, You have been victorious. When I have been blinded, You have brought revelation. When I have been chained, You have brought deliverance. Thank you, Father!

I rejoice for the provisions He granted as I embarked upon my journey to reveal, *my story*. Every need I encountered, He supplied. Many have spoken encouraging words or simply listened patiently as I spoke of my labors and challenges while writing this book. Thank you, for your love and support.

Robert and Susie Ursprung, my heart rejoices each time I reflect upon our bond in the Spirit through that first powerful encounter we shared regarding *my story*. Your prayers, wisdom, and kind words strengthened my resolve to press forward to be obedient to my Father, and my heart overflows with thankfulness and love.

To my pastor, Shane Gray, thank you, for undergirding me with the truth of God's word. I praise the Father for a man of God who, without fear, declares the whole counsel of God with love and compassion. Thank you, for loving Jesus above all else.

A warm, loving appreciation to my big sister, Joyce Avery, for your added clarification of some childhood memories. God protected us during some difficult days. I am exceedingly joyful for these last years we have shared. Thank you for your gentle heart, Sis, and for loving me.

My heart is full of love to my sons for their supply. Thank you, Matthew, Caleb, and Jacob, for providing me the computers which I used to accomplish my task. Your unselfishness gave me the opportunity to fulfill a call, by God, upon my heart.

My technical support team of my son-in-law Aubrey Boterf and sons Matthew and Caleb has been a gracious gift. Without you, I would have been lost in the world of technology, so endless thanks to you.

Becky Dillion, I am overwhelmed with the generosity of your heart to execute the editorial process of my manuscript. The editing process, which you accomplished with professional expertise, was a labor of love. With loving affection, I thank you, precious friend, and Sister in Christ, for making possible a more polished manuscript for publication.

I am indebted to you, Stephen Parks, State Law Librarian of the State Law Library of Mississippi, for your detailed, yet concise, instructions for each question I posed to you concerning the correct citing of trial transcripts.

To my former attorney, James Helveston, thank you, for the services you rendered to my family and me during some very dark days. I also appreciate you providing the documents I requested for my book. Your compassion that you extended to me until the end of my legal journey stirred my heart to deep gratitude. May God bless you.

Caleb, you deserve an additional accolade for your willingness to discharge, with competence, the undertaking of the publication of my book, *A Work of Lace*. Without your unselfish assistance and savvy, my manuscript would likely have died a slow death in the files of my computer. Your insight coupled with your excellence to complete a task confidently assured me that my book would roll off the press at the appointed time of the Father. With my heart full adoration, Caleb, I praise the Father for all of your help!

> *To everything there is a season, and a time to every purpose under the heaven: ... a time to keep silence, and a time to speak (Ecclesiastes 3:1,7bKJV).*

To my children, with unfeigned love, John, Amy, Matthew, Caleb, Rachel, Ruth, Joshua, Mary, and Jacob, you have been my heart in this journey, and I am awed and humbled to be your mother. You are the most overwhelming testimony that God had a plan and purpose for my life. I pray that the revelation of *my story* will magnify, for you, the beauty and power of His freedom through truth revealed.

Preface

Dear readers, those who struggle and those who are intimidated and fearful, may the unveiling of my anguish and devastation grant you the strength and courage to stand for truth in your heart, in your life, and in your pain. May this book inspire and compel hurting people in all walks of life to speak and not be silent. Someone will give you an audience, and someone will care about your devastation.

Mothers, you must embrace your duty to protect your children, to teach them to protect themselves against predators, and to alert them that the predator may be one who is supposed to guard and love them. Watch for the red flags warning of impending danger and listen to the still small voice whispering within your heart. If that still small voice makes utterances of unrest within your heart, upend the stone of silence, and address the unrest.

To better understand the unfolding of the catastrophic events my children and I suffered, I felt guided by the Lord to include a production of the memories of my childhood. A glimpse in retrospect will, I pray, enable you to have a more in-depth and unclouded view of *my story*. May the backdrop of my childhood memories facilitate the unraveling of the mysteries surrounding some of my actions and lack of actions during my adult life.

> *The human heart is the most deceitful of all things, and desperately wicked. Who really knows how bad it is (Jeremiah 17:9 NLT)?*

Introduction

The purposes for gathering my thoughts about my life and transforming those thoughts into a printed format are multiple. The most profound reason is an unrelenting impression from God to remove my veil and be transparent. I am convinced He wants me to share my tragedies and victories, so that light will be shed on truth and hope. I desire for hurting people to know that truth will set them free. You do not have to suffer in silence. Silence is your captor, and truth is your deliverer. If you have suffered or are suffering at the hands of another physically, verbally, mentally, sexually, or emotionally, I urge you to speak and not give the perpetrator control by being silent. Silence encourages the abuse to continue. The perpetrator is counting on your silence. Speak the truth about your suffering, and God will provide avenues of deliverance for you because He is the Deliverer.

This book addresses many of the personal tragedies I experienced during childhood and adulthood. Some of the issues presented in the following pages include sexual abuse, emotional abuse, physical abuse, manipulation, loss of self-worth, loss of identity, deception, and spiritual control. As *my story* unfolds throughout the progression of my life, you will be able to identify the preceding issues as they emerge in the scenes of life events. Although those issues were dark clouds in my life, they were overcome by the brightness of the Son. Deliverance found an avenue through truth unveiled.

The voice of a child speaks loudly to those who care. Mothers and Fathers, it is your God-given duty to protect your child. Instruction to your child concerning pedophiles is necessary to build a platform of safety regarding this area of abuse. Do not procrastinate or avoid your grave responsibility to cultivate safe boundaries. Negligence to train your child concerning sexual abuse could leave the door open to the possibility of horrific events. It is a great travesty to ignore the reality of pedophiliac abuse. Statistics explode with alarming facts about the frequency of these heinous acts. Do not hesitate to educate your child about the deception a pedophile incorporates and weaves into his approach and involvement as he targets an unsuspecting child. Teach your child that an abuser may be a person who is supposed to love and protect him. Expose evil and do not be afraid or embarrassed to teach your child to guard himself by telling others if someone hurts or confuses him in any way.

Never lose sight of who you were created to be because God made you an individual. You are responsible to protect that marvelous, authentic person God formed. Do not stumble into the pitfall of embracing propaganda that you are not a deserving or worthy person. Do not succumb to the lies of the father of all lies, Satan. Sometimes, he plants a negative thought in your mind about yourself. Dispel the thought for what it is—a lie from the great deceiver. God created you beautiful.

Remember, another person can never complete you. The idea of another person completing you is a worldly concept intertwined into the worldview of romance and love. Although this philosophy beckons us as it tickles our ears and strums on our heart strings, it is a false ideology. It is a lie of Satan. It is a distraction from the truth of God. Another person does not have the ability or the power to complete you. Delegating another the responsibility of your happiness is an unfair and weighty burden, which is destined for failure. Happiness comes and goes as circumstances fluctuate and change. Only joy will remain constant, and joy comes from God, not people. God is the only one who has the power and authority to make you complete and joyful.

And you are complete in Him…
(Colossians 2:10 KJV).
Our hearts ache, but we always have joy.
(II Corinthians 6:10 NLT).

An individual's relationship with God never depends on another person. A spiritual relationship is between God and the individual alone; therefore, you do not please God through another individual. A child of God's direct lifeline is to his Savior with no detours through another human. The veil of the temple of the Old Testament was rent from top to bottom when the perfect Lamb of God was sacrificed for our sins. The veil is forever gone. His sacrifice on the cross obtained direct access to God for us and signified that we do not have to go through another person to reach Him. Hebrews teaches us that we have a merciful and faithful high priest, who is the mediator of the new covenant. We have no need for a mediator in the flesh, for Christ is our mediator.

Always remember *truth,* not silence. If I am transparent to others about the devastating events that occurred in my life, they will be able to translate *my story* as one of hope and victory. God may use my transparency to speak to you and open the eyes of your understanding to the truth wherein you abide. Yes, I was a victim at one time, but by the power and grace of God I have risen out of ashes to beauty.

To appoint them that morn in Zion, to give them beauty for ashes, the oil of joy for morning, the garment of praise for the spirit of heaviness, that they might be called trees of righteousness, the planting of the Lord, that He might be glorified. (Isaiah 61:3).

Lord, I commend this work unto You. Be Thou glorified!

A Work of Lace

In the recesses of my mind,
Stands an ordinary, white clapboard find.

Curly-haired lass with her brother and sister did dwell,
Amidst the meadows in the green and grassy dell.

Many emotions and events played out in this place,
Each emotion and event was woven to form an indelible,
unalterable lace.

Lace that is sometimes imported and so costly it is forbidden,
Other times the lace is worn, tattered, and hidden.

Marvelous it would be to bury the worn and tattered in a chest,
And only display the finest and best.

Oh! not so—For it is the whole woven work of lace,
That does make the person these words embrace.

—Betty Vaden

Life can be compared to a work of lace. The weaver takes ordinary, unassuming thread and weaves or *works* it into an intricate, connected pattern transforming the thread into an extraordinarily beautiful creation known as lace. He fashions his design with countless stitches, and each stitch of the lace is fundamental to reveal the desired pattern or finished work. Sometimes a work of lace may become stained or tattered and worn by the rigors of use. Likewise, our lives are fashioned as each event and emotion is woven together to form an intricate, connected pattern. Even the tiniest event of our lives is crucial to form the finished pattern. We experience times of weeping as well as times of rejoicing throughout our lives in the process of weaving our work of lace. Eternity will reveal the Master Weaver's wonderful plan of grace and mercy in each of His children's lives. The glorious beauty of our lives will exalt Him when He reveals His unfathomable *work of lace* in us.

Early Beginnings on the Farm

In the northwest corner of Tennessee, amid the rolling hills of the fertile farmland of Henry County, stood an ordinary white clapboard dwelling. Happy memories as well as dark memories transpired in this place. James Foster Smyth, his wife, Sue Jane Kilgore Smyth, and their three children identified this dwelling as home. I was the baby girl, and Daddy called me Betty Sue after Mother. My older sibling, whom I held in great awe, answered to Brenda Joyce. My brother, the middle child, bore mother's maiden name Kilgore and was named James Kilgore.

Our country farmhouse, with gingerbread trim, sat atop a gently sloping plot of land and was adorned by rose bushes and other flowering bushes like forsythia, lilac, and althea. As the front yard sloped toward the gravel road, it was dotted with jewels of assorted bulbs that greeted us in early spring. Mother had collected brilliantly yellow buttercups from her childhood home place and had transplanted them around the yard's front perimeter. Various colors of dainty hyacinths released their sweet fragrance as they joined the floral chorus. As a little girl, I loved playing in the grass among the spring flowers. I thought the rainbow of flowers was such a treasure. I did not know why, but those little jewels of flowers stirred imaginations of great riches as I frolicked among them. Huge oaks stood loftily gracing the right corner of the yard in front of the house. Two pecan trees spread their branches over the yard closest to the driveway as it made the turn toward the house. We children gathered pecans that had fallen from those trees for Mother to use in some of her scrumptious homemade desserts.

The side entrance to the house was the door most of us, including visitors, frequented since our driveway ended at that portion of the house. Directly to the right of this side entrance was a splendid flower bed that Mother tended ever so lovingly. In the midst of her garden of flowers, rose a cistern, which was capped with a container that provided a place of display for flowering spring and summer annuals. Those rewards of the garden season flowed over the edge of the container and trickled down the sides of the whitewashed cistern. In late winter, Mother could be spotted with her eyes and thoughts fixated on the pages within the garden and seed catalogs. She carefully made decisions about the plants and seeds that would find lodging in her prized garden the following spring. Mother's tender touch and diligent labor in her flower garden produced a stunning landscape, which filled the country air with sweet fragrances.

Heading out the back door, a short jaunt away, was the vegetable garden spot. Our farmhand, Frank, walked behind the mule-pulled plow in early spring to turn up the earth in preparation for the planting of the garden. Gazing to the left of the back door, the silhouette of a crab apple tree appeared. Sometimes, I grabbed the saltshaker, headed to the crab apple tree, and pulled a small sour apple to munch. The red oil painted hen house with the chicken yard, where a rooster strutted around while clucking chickens scratched the earth, could also be spied from the small back porch. When the back door was opened, kitty cats would scatter from the little porch.

Farther back and to the right of the house stood the tool shed with its tin roof. Treasured childhood memories were captured when I escaped to the tool shed during brisk summer rains and listened as the flood of raindrops collided with the tin roof. Many small pieces of farm equipment plus a huge red Farmall tractor could easily be viewed in the open bay tool shed. A combine, a hay baler, and a corn picker constituted a list of enormous pieces of farm machinery which also found lodging in the tool shed. On the right end of the tool shed was the abundantly equipped shop with scads of tools including a welding machine and a huge vice grip. Positioned across the back wall of the shop was a large worktable. The open front tool shed was immense and everything in it was in full view of anyone who drove down the dusty, gravel road in front of our house. I did not think about the position or design of the tool shed as a young child, but as I got older I was embarrassed that everything in the tool shed could be seen by all who came to the house or drove down the dusty, gravel road. The tool shed had been constructed for function and convenience, not aesthetic purposes, or principles.

A corncrib had been erected a short distance behind the tool shed. The corncrib, which stored a portion of the fall harvest of corn, doubled as one of my escapes as a young girl. This rustic building provided a perfect refuge to live out and develop some of my inherent, God-given gifts of creativity and design. I loved playing in the vacant side of the corncrib and the grassy, shaded area directly in front of it, creating playhouses and furnishings to use in the playhouses. On the farm, I had the freedom to play and envision as my imagination took its natural course, and the corncrib was one of my workshops. Mother told me that I spent more time creating and building than I spent playing, but the imagining and designing were the parts in which I delighted and flourished. Those parts *were* play to me.

Completing the homestead landscape was the whitewashed painted dairy barn and two additional barns. The milk barn sat to the right of the tool shed; however, it was positioned much closer to the road. A pond for the livestock was situated a short distance to the left of the milk barn. It is gross and almost unimaginable that, as a child, I sometimes played in that pond. A towering red hay barn and a white stock barn with a white silo were located behind the dairy barn. The pond and these buildings were positioned within a fenced area, which kept the Jersey and Holstein cows hemmed in when they were brought from the pasture to the barn for milking. Daddy had a gas pump that was connected to a buried tank of colored gas used for fueling the tractor and farm trucks. The pump was near the dairy barn and gave the similitude of a bona fide gas pump (minus a brand name) at the local country store. During the winter months, the cows relied on the silage from the silo for food. They sought refuge and warmth in the stock barn, where the silage was dispersed from the adjacent silo. Two hundred plus acres of prime farmland stretched out behind our house and farm buildings providing acreage for crops as well as pasture for livestock to graze. This idyllic setting was where Mother and Daddy brought me as a newborn from the Nobles Memorial Hospital in nearby Paris, Tennessee. From infancy through my early teens, this was simply my home. A huge block of my memory is attributed to the events and daily routines that transpired in or near this place.

Imprinted on the pages of my mental scrapbook are snapshots of fear and uncertainty that had an onset in my early childhood. My daddy's prevailing personality personified an introvert; however, he transformed into a wild man while he staggered about in an inebriated state. When I was as young as three years old, memories of violence Daddy inflicted upon Mother were engraved upon my memory file. Often, she could be found weeping as she sat in the old jute bottom rocking chair, where she had nurtured us babies, because of physical and emotional pain that had been unleashed by the hand of drunken rage. One time, I discovered a butcher knife under my mother's pillow, and she explained to me that she had put the knife there to protect herself. Visions of scuffling, crying, and loud arguing would envelope my entire world as my daddy violently acted out while he weaved about in his drunken stupor. Many years later, after my sister and I had arrived in our golden years, she related an incident she remembered during one of Daddy's fits of rage toward Mother. My sister communicated that Mother was crumpled on the floor because Daddy had attacked her with a broken beer bottle. She covered Mother's body with her own small body to stop Daddy from continuing his attack. While a young child, my brave sister fiercely protected our sweet mother. Joyce's memory of the incident is overwhelmingly sad but demonstrated her fearless courage to shield Mother from additional harm. Daddy sometimes ordered Mother to take us kids to her parents' home to stay, so he could have some sort of drinking parties. What transpired at those parties remains a mystery; I only know he did not want us children present.

Great anxiety engulfed my emotional and mental state if Daddy had been drinking before we began our journey home from the town of Paris. Our farmhouse was about fifteen miles away in the rural community of Cottage Grove. This emotion of fear was overwhelming and paralyzing to me as a young child. The fear presented itself in my physical posture as I sat crouched and trembling on the edge of the backseat of the car. I would peer over the front seat to watch for the huge curve in the road referred to as the Booey curve. In my childish mind, I thought if we could just make it around that curve, then we would arrive home safely. These glimpses into my childhood memories illuminate a few of the terrifying moments attached to my daddy's unpredictable and brutal behavior when he had been overtaken by alcohol.

Even in the shadow of his alcoholism, Daddy's earning power was realized. He was a farmer by trade raising mostly corn, soybeans, and some type of suitable grass for hay. He rented his tobacco and cotton allotments to a family who lived on our farm. Daddy also operated a custom farming business, which provided a substantial portion of his capital. With financial backing supplied by his mother, Daddy purchased the most modern farm equipment available in advance of neighboring farmers. His possession of this equipment enabled him to service other farms as well as his own farm. Through this custom farming business, he generated a significant cash flow that filled in the gaps from planting time until harvest time of his crops. Possessing an aptitude of a mechanical genius, Daddy repaired most of his farm equipment, thereby, equipping him to a greater degree to succeed in his farming operation. Although he had those advantages, there was one snag— his alcohol dependency. Much work would be scheduled and accomplished, but when he collected his fee, the profits seldom provided sustenance or comfort for his family. The power of his alcohol dependency always seemed to prevail. The revenues would be consumed by the purchase of more alcohol, the participation in gambling, the carousing with immoral women, and the other related lifestyle practices of an alcoholic. Our family's only other source of income was profits derived from the dairy farm business. Due to my daddy's addiction, the brunt of the dairy farm business fell upon my mother's weary shoulders.

My mother was a gentle, kind-hearted soul and a diligent, persevering laborer. She raised three children, maintained a rambling country farmhouse, tended a large vegetable garden (preserved the bounty), participated in church activities, and engaged in our school and community functions. In addition to these responsibilities, she managed to be the in-charge person for the dairy cow portion of the farm. Mother's position to oversee the dairy farm was demanding and time consuming. One requirement of operating a dairy farm was that the cows had to be brought to the milk barn twice daily to be milked. She arose in the darkness and often battled inclement weather as her duties with the first milking commenced. Late afternoon was the final milking of the day. Milking cows was confining and regimented. It did not matter what other duties or plans ensued throughout the day, because the milking of the cows was the priority. Milking cows was a methodical and time sensitive chore. Mother could not slack on the commitment, for she knew that our livelihood was dependent on the income derived from the cows. In addition, the cows' utters and sacks had to be relieved twice daily to enable them to continue producing milk and to prevent problems for the cows.

My grade schoolteachers always desired to have my mother as their class mother. They knew they could depend upon Mother to bake a delicious cake for a cake walk, to write a play for the class to present, or to support her children as well as other children in whatever way that was needed. She personified a compassionate, generous spirit. As I reflect on my childhood, I am amazed with the recollection of the volume of tasks and volunteering Mother accomplished. She succeeded in the daunting, seemingly impossible amount of responsibilities and volunteering, and she did it with joy and without complaint.

While an elementary student, I became quite ill with some type of kidney problem which required complete bed rest. I missed school for several weeks because of my confinement to bed. Mother, endeavoring to bring her little girl some cheer from the sick bed, took a break from her impossible schedule to sew some doll clothes for me. I distinctly recall one of the garments she fashioned was a little white coat with bright pink flowers on it. She made the doll clothes completely from her imagination and God-given talents as she had zero doll clothes' patterns. The gifts and diversity of this woman were astounding, and she continually gave of herself to her children as well as others.

Mother's parents, who the grandchildren referred to as Ma and Pap, lived in a rural community located in adjoining Weakly

County. Their house was about fifteen miles away from our farm in Henry County over winding, gravel roads. My grandparents lived a meager lifestyle and resided in a small weathered-wood house. It was located on a picturesque, dusty lane which curved away from the main road as it made its ascent. The trees' branches intertwined overhead, and grass appeared in the middle of the narrow, recluse passageway as the lane curved. The lane was not surfaced with any gravel; therefore, it was not always worthy of travel during the rainy or snowy winter months of Tennessee.

The bathroom facility was located outside the perimeters of the house in an outhouse. Plumbing was nonexistent, and there were no porcelain or acrylic bathroom fixtures in the outhouse. The Sears and Roebuck catalog pages were the Charmin tissue of the day. I thought it was grand to venture outside to go potty even though the nearby air was saturated with unpleasant odors. Since the house lacked plumbing, a portable enamel bucket was available if anyone needed to go to the bathroom during the darkness of the night.

The water well was just a few steps from the back door. Fresh, cold water was drawn from the well in a long tubular apparatus and released into an oak bucket to take inside for drinking, cooking, and household purposes. I was so intrigued by the well and the drawing of the water. My grandmother would, very hesitantly, let me draw the water from time-to-time. I loved to lean over the top of the well and project my voice into the well cavity and listen for the echo. There was a three-foot upright earthen pottery type structure that enclosed the well opening. Ma emphatically cautioned me to be careful as I let the cylinder down into the well. You had to lower the cylinder, ever so slowly, and listen for it to bubble as the bubbling sound indicated it was full and ready to be retrieved. If one lowered the cylinder too quickly, it could touch the bottom of the well and stir up the sand. Whoever made this mistake was in big trouble. Then, you would have to wait until the sand settled and the water cleared before trying again. That was dismaying news, for it meant no water in the old oak bucket which clearly indicated no water at all. A little table, which sat just inside the back door, was the resting place for the water bucket. What fun it was to get a drink from the old oak bucket using the dipper. Drinking from the dipper was a form of simple entertainment for the young grandchildren scampering around the yard and house. I thought it was absolutely the best tasting water I had ever drunk.

I can remember carefree times at Ma and Pap's with my many cousins as we gathered around Ma's table. At mealtime, the children would line up on a bench at the table, which was always covered with a red and white checked pattern oilcloth tablecloth. The table sat in the kitchen along with the wood stove and a real old-timey icebox. The icebox was replaced with a small electric refrigerator, and the wood stove gave way to an apartment size electric stove during my childhood. The only heat in the old house was an open fireplace or grate as we referred to it. We gathered around the fireplace and warmed ourselves facing frontwards. Likewise, we turned around and warmed our backsides as we faced outward. You were freezing on one side and blistering hot on the other side.

While I was a child, Ma and Pap sometimes visited our house and stayed for a few days. They did not own a vehicle, so mother would go get them whenever they visited. If we drove into town for supplies, Mother and Ma did the shopping. I was frequently designated to abide with Pap to pass time in town while they did the shopping. Leaving me to fend for myself, Pap often went into a place that we referred to as a beer joint (I guess it was somewhat of a crude forerunner of a bar.) to drink alcohol. He told me not to mention to Mother that he had been drinking or that he had been inside the beer joint. His drinking or his instruction for me to lie for him, however, was not the worse memory of emotional trauma Pap inflicted upon me as a trusting child of her granddaddy. He delivered a very dark moment unto me. One who was supposed to be a protector of me took advantage of my innocence. This ungodly, dark secret was a memory that I kept buried in the chambers of my mind for many, many years. My granddaddy sexually molested me as I sat in his lap one evening in our front yard. I was about five years old and had fallen asleep in his lap. I awoke to the horror of his perverted deed. I felt deep shame and betrayal as a young child, and I never spoke of the incident to him, Mother, or anyone. Decades passed before I talked about his ungodly deed. Not telling anyone and pretending it never happened made it seem less upsetting and real. I thought I had achieved this place of complacency within my subconscious until another tragedy engulfed my world years later. This ungodly secret betrayal delivered by my granddaddy stayed buried in my mind for more than fifty years.

As life unfolded in the mundane and humble day-to-day routine, my hurting and disillusioned child's heart longed for a transformation in our home. My most intense desire was to have what I imagined my friends enjoyed; a secure, happy refuge void of turmoil and fear. A home founded on the grace of God and centered in serving Him was my ever-present yearning. Mother was hesitant to allow me to invite friends from school or church. She sometimes, although reluctantly, caved to my pleas. Her love for me and her efforts to afford me simple childhood pleasures, occasionally, swayed her better judgment. It was in those tender, vulnerable moments that I was permitted to have playmates visit. She worked tirelessly trying to provide a loving atmosphere and to make home a happy place. We, however, primarily existed day-to-day in the anxiety of Daddy having one of his drunken fits of rage.

Although we lived in this glass house of the constant apprehension of a vile outburst from Daddy, Mother was committed to serving God. From her strong faith and devotion to God, sprang a dedication to teach and to train her children to walk in the paths of righteousness. She faithfully took us children to church at the Cottage Grove Baptist Church, where I basked in the safe environment of the church. The comfort and abiding peace I found at God's house provided me a place of sanctuary. Daddy tormented Mother emotionally and verbally for her dedication to the Lord and for her persistence of our church attendance. He made all manner of sorted accusations toward Mother about the church, the pastor, or the people who comprised the membership. She bravely took the harsh, wounding words that were sometimes accompanied with physical abuse. Mother refused to allow his threats or actions to deter her commitment to Christ or her responsibility to her children regarding spiritual matters.

After participating in vacation Bible school one summer, we looked forward to the classic closing-day picnic scheduled for the final Friday. Well, Daddy had been on one of his boozing binges and did not arrive home in his truck until late. We had to wait until he arrived home to go to the picnic as his truck was our only mode of transportation. Mother rushed to get us to the picnic on time. Her rushing made the drive on the gravel road somewhat precarious. She hit a bumpy part of the gravel road, commonly referred to as a washboard, and lost control of the truck. We ended up teetering on a peninsula-like portion of dirt in a deep ravine. My brother hit the windshield, since there were no seatbelts then, and cut his chin; thus, he had to be taken to the hospital for stitches. Everyone else was physically okay, but we were emotional basket cases. As a little girl, all I comprehended was that due to my daddy's drinking another childhood experience had been stolen from me.

I dreamed of Daddy becoming a Christian which in my thoughts equated with us attending church as a family. To have this God-centered home was an ultimate strong desire that was birthed in my childhood and abode in my heart throughout my life on the farm. After the cows had been milked one Sunday, Daddy came inside, bathed, and dressed. And that night seemed as if a miracle were unfolding because we all went to church together. Even though, he had made a profession of faith and had been baptized during his younger years, he came forward at the close of the service that night. The pastor related that Daddy had made a confession and rededication. My heart sang within my chest, for I thought my dream of a peaceful and secure home environment was about to be realized. My dream, however, was soon crushed. The Smyth family's life continued in the same melancholy, dismal pattern as it always had. Daddy's reformation faded, and he continued down the path of alcoholism and wasted living.

Although the knowledge of Daddy's alcoholism was widespread throughout the area, the Smyth family name and reputation were held in honorable esteem. If an assessment of the Smyth's respectability from the residents of Henry County had been polled, I believe it would have revealed a consensus that the Smyth's represented a good family background. This consensus would have been largely due to my hard working, financially successful, entrepreneurially spirited grandmother Jessie Kate Mills Smyth. She and Vernon Moore Smyth were the parents of three boys, C.D., James (my daddy), and Marvin. During the childhood years and the young adulthood of their three boys, my grandparents owned and operated a farm in Henry County, Tennessee. It was the same farm where Mother and Daddy brought me as an infant, and where I spent my childhood and the beginning of my teen years.

My grandmother's first dabbling in the business world was the merchandising of fresh eggs, milk, butter, and cream from their farm. From these humble beginnings, she managed to buy hundreds of acres of prime farmland in Henry County. Her next maneuver in the business world was to launch her own professional milk pasteurizing business. Her establishment of a dairy pasteurizing processing plant was a pioneer of its time in a small town of West Tennessee. Until my grandmother (a woman who broke a few glass ceilings in her generation) orchestrated her pasteurizing business in Paris, the facilities had been in larger, distant cities. The name of her business venture was Paris Dairy.

When my grandmother launched Paris Dairy, she and Granddaddy owned and occupied a house in Paris on Caldwell Avenue. The house was on the same street as the business and was a lovely two-story tannish blonde brick structure. The exterior design of the front facade featured a spacious portico with brick walls designed with large arched openings. To approach the porch, one would ascend several concrete steps, which were flanked by stately ferns on each side. Another veranda, with an entry the family used to access the home, was on the right side of the house. Next to this porch were lovely blue hydrangea bushes. Both porches were adorned with large metal porch gliders and relaxing chairs, which as a young child, I thought only the rich could possibly own.

The interior of the house was decorated with ornately carved mahogany wood furnishings, intricately patterned blue wool rugs, and sumptuous brocade upholstered pieces. Beautiful lamps, pictures, and accessories embellished each room throughout the lovely home. One lamp that sat on an exquisite sofa table in the living room's boxed bay area was especially alluring and captivated my attention. It featured a splotchy decorated rectangular shade in hues of golden browns and was the final touch of the three-pronged candlestick burnished brass lamp.

I loved spending time at my grandmother's. She kept sliced ham and pimento cheese for sandwiches in her Kelvinator refrigerator. On the red and chrome table of the kitchen dinette set was always a box of store-bought, assorted cookies. These were goodies that I was not accustomed to having on the farm. Everything we ate on the farm was homemade, so I thought anything store-bought was a special treat. Her bedroom had comfy, upholstered chairs, and the room also functioned as a sitting room for family. The room had a mantle where she had positioned a mantle clock. Whether sitting in one of the chairs or talking to her on the phone, I heard the distinct ticking of that clock. It etched a memory in my mind that caused me to associate the sound of mantle clocks with my grandmother.

For several years, my grandmother managed the prosperous dairy business known as Paris Dairy. She marketed milk, chocolate milk, old-fashioned boiled custard, ice cream, cottage cheese, and other associated dairy products. The recipes for several of the products were her own culinary creations. She named the ice cream after her first grandchild, dubbing it Mary Lynn ice cream. During the early 1950s, it was relatively novel to produce the pasteurized milk in the same vicinity as local farms that supplied the raw milk. The dairy products were merchandized in supermarkets in Paris and neighboring towns as well as offered for home delivery in Paris. Yes, the milk was distributed in glass bottles and was delivered to many doors of Paris, Tennessee, residents. Each year she published a large milk bottle shaped calendar, which featured a picture of one of her grandchildren. I was thrilled when my picture appeared as the new calendar girl. In my childish understanding, my grandmother was wealthy and could afford to spoil me and lavish me with my heart's desire.

Bebe was my grandmother's pet name by the grandchildren. She delighted her sons and their families with her generosity. This generosity, however, was the stimulus of much jealously and strife among family members. Each time she bestowed some act of unselfishness toward one family member, then, other family members would demand something. She was constantly trying to maintain balance with her acts of benevolence.

My grandmother's business savvy enabled her to acquire multiple properties in Paris and hundreds of acres of farmland in Henry County in addition to the prosperous dairy business. She proved to be a capable businesswoman in an era when a woman's place was not in the forefront of the business world. The reality that Bebe financially secured each of her son's homes and farms could be attributed to her charitable spirit, but this spirit was sometimes coupled with a controlling reign. All three of her sons depended on her financially and emotionally to some degree. Consequently, due to her strong personality traits she controlled them in some respects. She must have concluded that her actions were the most beneficial and prudent way to prosper them and their families. It is impossible, however, to use power and money to make others happy or content. Unless controlled by the grace of God, the appetites of the flesh are never satisfied and continue to be greedy and selfish. The Smyth family unit was not exempt from this flaw of greed. My grandmother's loving and unselfish heart was trampled upon by her family's unrelenting covetousness. She loved her family and desired to bless them with the bounty that God had supplied through her diligence, but they took advantage of her generosity.

During my childhood, Bebe represented the financial pinnacle of the fulfillment of my hopes and dreams in the realm of material possessions. My comprehension of her capability to buy things for me was that she endeavored to demonstrate her love through the bestowing of things. My grandmother's ability to reward my childhood fantasies was the reality of one of my obsessions. I do not remember how she was aware of my obsession, but she knew. Horses had become my madness during my youth. Two of my country friends had horses, so I thought I also had to have one. Bebe instructed me to find a good horse for her to purchase. With Mother directing the pursuit, the search ensued. We located the personification of perfect horse flesh that met my grandmother's approval. I was ecstatic when my horse was transported to the farm. Dan was a real beauty; he sported a shiny sorrel color coat, four white-stocking feet, and a white blaze down his face. Dan and I had many wonderful times roaming the sprawling acres of our farm. Sometimes, my friends would meet me on the dusty, gravel roads of Cottage Grove, and we would gallop off to some childhood escape. In addition to traveling to each other's farms, one time we met and rode our horses to the annual fair held at Cottage Grove School where we attended. Our horses were our avenues of adventure, affording us somewhat of an independence at a tender age.

During the summer months of school vacation, I arose early in the cool of the day to perform my designated chore. Dan my horse, Bimbo our black and white shepherd dog, and I would head to the pasture to round up the cows for the first milking. I hated to get up early, but I loved the cool, refreshing air afforded one on a summer's day during that unconventional hour. I was fascinated and amused as I watched an untrained Bimbo nip at the heels of the milk cows while guiding them toward the direction of the barn. He was a real natural. There was an audible call I projected to the cows that wooed them in my direction. Dan, Bimbo, and I were quite a remarkable threesome as we performed as ranchers on our farm.

About the time I was preteen, BeBe presented me with a beautiful solid maple bookcase bedroom suite. I just knew that I was surly the richest girl in my world. I floated upward and landed on good 'ole cloud nine when the Baxter Clark Furniture truck ambled down the dusty, gravel road and delivered my bedroom furniture to rural route three. The delivery men carried the furniture to my room upstairs, and I was dazzled. I had pure pleasure situating all my stuff in my bedroom that day. Probably, fifty years later, after serving me in my youth and beginning years of my marriage, that same bedroom furniture was used by some of my grandchildren.

BeBe desired to expose her grandchildren to the cultural aspect of life by encouraging and financing some type of music lessons for all of us who would embrace the opportunity. Some of the grandchildren tried voice and dance, while others ventured in different musical directions. Her appreciation for the finer things in life prompted her to guide us to explore the possibility of developing an undiscovered talent. Some of us grandchildren chose piano lessons as our window of opportunity. She must have hoped for an outstanding gift to be realized. Although she never lived to see his piano accomplishments, one of Uncle Marvin's sons did become a concert pianist. Well, yours truly did not make the grade; practice got the best of me. On second thought, maybe it was Miss Dolly Crutchfield, my strict second-grade piano teacher, who got the best of me. Nevertheless, middle C was about the total of what I recalled of my musical endeavors.

When I was about nine years old, Mother separated from Daddy with BeBe acting as the financial silent partner. We children moved with Mother to live in Chattanooga, Tennessee, where one of her older brothers resided. We occupied the upstairs of the house where he and his family lived. The downstairs was one rental, and the upstairs was a separate rental with an outside entry. I was overjoyed to move and have a new beginning, but this great aspiration of new beginnings was soon dashed. Mother, having only finished the ninth grade, was unable to find employment. Daddy came to Chattanooga with promises of reform and persuaded Mother to go back to the farm; hence, back we trudged to Cottage Grove.

During my childhood, an idea stuck in my mind that possibly BeBe may have thought Mother contributed to Daddy's alcohol problems. My perceived thought pattern of her attributing blame toward Mother seemed to be the basis for a chasm that developed within our family. I had another idea that maybe Mother had not met BeBe's expectations concerning the standard of a prominent family background. Whatever the cause, Mother and my grandmother had some sort of disenchantment or falling out with one another. Mother ceased to visit at BeBe and Granddaddy's, and a strained unspoken rift seemed to erect an invisible wall between them. I am not sure this wall was ever toppled.

Experiencing the instability of an alcoholic daddy, who did not adequately provide for his family financially, emotionally, or spiritually instilled within me with an immense feeling of insecurity and low self-esteem. No memories lodged in my mental file of any engaging or supportive conversations with my daddy throughout my childhood and early teen years. No remembrances of any hugs or endearing words like "I love you" lingered. His inability to display affection and engage in a warm daddy and daughter relationship with me was a catalyst for my feelings of unworthiness. At a young age, I began to strive for acceptance in all areas of my life. I began to exemplify a consuming determination to achieve success and approval. Whenever I attended Sunday school, vacation Bible school, or other church events, I always wanted to be assigned the longest Bible verse to memorize or have the most difficult part to prepare for any special program. I desired to be recognized and accepted. I believe I substituted my achievement in these religious programs to help fulfill a need that I had longed for from my emotionally absent father. Perfection or at least high achievement also became a priority in my schoolwork.

During my first nine grades of school, one of my childhood friends and I competed for the highest grades. On one occasion, I decided to remain in study hall and work on Algebra while the rest of the study hall class was dismissed to a nice spring day of softball. Since I was a focused and driven individual, who endeavored to hone a certain level of perfection, I often exercised the tool of self-discipline. I desired the support and recognition of my teachers and was determined to prove to everyone that I could achieve success. I longed to rise above the veil of degradation that surrounded our family because of Daddy's alcoholism. I was ashamed that Daddy was a drunk, so I aspired to prove to my world that my life would be different. I was determined to conqueror my mountain associated with academic achievement.

On the contrary, my brother Jimmie did not seem to share my aspirations to separate from the dark clouds of Daddy's alcoholism. He began indulging in the use of alcohol during his teenage years and demonstrated a rebellious spirit to Mother's authority. When he was ready to begin eighth grade, my grandmother made a deal with him. She persuaded him to attend Castle Heights Military Academy, which was a two to three hour's drive from the farm. I do not know what she initiated as leverage to sway him to comply but comply he did. I am sure it was her great hope that the atmosphere and strong discipline abiding within the military academy would transform and subdue Jimmie. I believe my grandmother earnestly desired for Jimmie to avoid falling prey to alcoholism as Daddy had. Bebe loved her grandchildren and reached out to intercede for them and protect them.

I do not recall any distinct change in Jimmie after his Castle Heights' experience that exemplified that he had been transformed into a more compliant individual. He drank alcohol and ran wild with girls during high school; although, he did graduate. Jimmie was a smart and creative young man, but he was not interested in achieving a high level of performance with his education. One time, I asked him why he drank when he knew how alcohol had destroyed our home. Silence was my answer. Later in life, I witnessed alcohol snuff out the candle of his life at the young age of fifty-two. My heart was deeply saddened that my brother had been unable to grasp or overcome the devastation alcohol dependency caused. Daddy also suffered a premature death at age forty due to long years of alcohol abuse.

Another time that my grandmother intervened in my family was regarding my older sister, Joyce. Daddy mistreated my big sister with harsh discipline coupled with demeaning attitudes and actions. Joyce sought refuge with our grandmother, who had a soft heart toward us grandchildren and would not tolerate our mistreatment. She traveled with BeBe and Granddaddy to Arizona and lived with them during the time she was a teenager. My granddaddy suffered many years with severe asthma; therefore, he followed the advice of his physician and moved to the hot, dry climate of Arizona seeking relief. After living there for a little longer than a year, Joyce and my grandmother returned to Paris while Granddaddy remained a bit longer in Arizona. She continued to live with BeBe away from the farm. That summer, Joyce began working in Paris at a classy hotel restaurant, The Greystone. She met her future husband Chuck while waiting tables in the hotel restaurant. He was a paratrooper stationed at Fort Campbell Army Base about sixty miles away near Clarksville, Tennessee.

After Joyce's sixteenth birthday, she and Chuck married in a lovely ceremony at my grandmother's house. Their first child was born the second year they were married. When we went to visit Joyce in the hospital at Fort Campbell Army Base, following the birth of their baby girl, I pointed out a sign in the hospital to Mother. The sign stated no visitors under the age of sixteen would be allowed in the maternity ward. I giggled and commented that Joyce barely made it into the hospital ward. My big sister was married by the time I was about eleven. I missed her and had always thought she was tops even though she would chase me out of her room if she caught me meddling with her stuff. You know, she was my big sister, and I considered everything that she did awesome and grand.

My grandmother employed me to clean her house the year before her death. I went to her house once a week to perform the task. She loved me coming to clean and remarked that her house always reflected when I had been there. One Saturday when I went to clean, I discovered her in bed asleep. Later that day, I heard that she had been taken for emergency care due to an overdose of an antidepressant medication. Guilt flooded me because I had not recognized that she was in a desperate medical situation instead of sleeping. I never knew whether her overdose was accidental or intentional.

In my understanding, my grandmother was tormented by the curse of overwhelming depression during the last few years of her life. Shortly before her death, she confided to me that the family would be better off if she were dead. Her mind set was that the family would have her money if she died. I reassured her that was not the case and that I loved her. As a teenager, I did not grasp the gravity of her words or mental state. How sad to think my grandmother's thoughts were so dismal and influenced by the evil forces of the master liar Satan. Deliverance was needed for my grandmother to have had power over the dark forces of evil, which manipulated her thoughts. Within a short time following that comment to me, Aunt Lila's husband, Uncle Tom, found my grandmother's lifeless body in the separate garage behind her house. The powers of darkness, the disappointments of life, and the misuse of antidepressant medications culminated in her early, self-initiated death. The Bible labels the battle in which Christians engage as a spiritual war. Ephesians states that the war we fight is not against flesh and blood, but … against spiritual wickedness in high places. We must put on the entire armor of God to be victorious. I was devastated by the loss of my grandmother.

Due to her suicide, I experienced a self-inflicted feeling of embarrassment. The forces of evil and the powers of darkness were bombarding my thoughts and perceptions following her death. One of my cousins and I went to get a fountain drink at one of the local drugstores shortly after her death. I felt as if everyone's eyes in the drugstore were focused on me and mesmerized by my presence. My heart pounded within my chest, and my face flushed. I felt hot and faint. Whether real or imagined, my initial impulse was to flee the scene of scrutiny. The cloak of low self-esteem covered me and lied to me with shrieking screams and bursts of humiliating taunts. It seemed that it had wrapped around me in such a smothering manner that I felt as if my very breath were about to be snuffed out as candle on a dark, windy night.

I was a junior in high school at the time of my grandmother's death. My existing low self-esteem sank a few notches lower following her death. With the appearance of each family tragedy, I sank lower into my pit of worthlessness. In my mind, I had become a magnet that attracted and bore the reproach of my grandmother's tragic death as well as my daddy's addiction to alcohol. I assumed the reproach of each adverse family trial as if it were my own. I was ashamed for my friends and classmates to know the details of my grandmother's death. Since I lived in a small Southern town, it was inevitable to avoid the news and cause of her death. An article appeared in the local Paris newspaper publishing the fact of her death as well as the circumstances surrounding it.

Moving to Town and Crossing Boundaries

During the summer before I started the ninth grade, Mother decided to leave daddy. Preparation was critical to ensure that leaving Daddy and the farm would be successful. Our summer was dedicated to canning and freezing as much food from the garden as possible. Mother did not discuss with me how our financial needs would be provided after we moved. I did not know if she had saved money or if my grandmother had provided financial assistance. Mother formulated a strategy to pursue her GED; then, she planned to enroll in a LPN nursing class. Following our move, Mother followed through with a divorce. I felt an immense surge of relief come over me as I realized that I would no longer face the tumult, anxiety, or embarrassment of Daddy's irrational and violent outbursts prompted by his alcoholism.

Mother, my brother, and I made the move from the farm into town to live in a house my grandmother owned. I thought the house was beautiful and exceeded the clapboard farmhouse. I was so excited about the move and realized city life would be a contrast to the life I had been accustomed. City life would eliminate the status quo associated with the farm, and there would be no more rounding up the milk cows, no more sprawling country landscapes, no more garden produce to preserve, no more yellow school bus rides, and no more gravel roads. I was elated and felt that we had moved up in the world. The house was a two-story burgundy brick, which featured a curved front porch graced with a swing on the portion that wrapped around to the side of the house. A Victorian black iron fence provided a decorative separation of the property and the sidewalk. The stately and intricately carved front door was embellished with a full-length oval beveled glass.

Upon entering the front door, beautiful parquet wood floors could be noted. The living room boasted a fireplace complimented by a lovely mantel. The front two rooms were large with twelve to fifteen-foot ceilings adorned with brass light fixtures and brass crown molding. For my bedroom, I was appointed the large front room to the right of the living room. It could be concealed by shutting enormous double doors. By its location and design, it appeared that the original function of my room had been an elaborate dining room. The golden sunlight flooded the room through huge windows, casting a lovely glow on the polished floors. I was jubilant. All the downstairs rooms were spacious with those skyscraper high ceilings.

Mother possessed the ingenuity to create a cozy and inviting decor within the house, accomplishing a homey atmosphere. She hung sheer, white ruffled tiebacks on the windows of my bedroom. As a fourteen-year-old ninth grader, I beautified the room with my girly trappings. I loaded the shelf of my maple bookcase bed with my stuffed animals, and I flounced a white chenille bedspread on the bed as the crowning touch. Above the bed, I hung the little white framed ballerina pictures that once belonged to my big sister, Joyce. In one corner of the room, I positioned my huge oak desk. I spent hours concentrating at my desk as I studied for those coveted high scores to succeed academically.

Jimmy and I commuted with our principal to continue our education at Cottage Grove School the first year we lived in town. It was Jimmy's senior year, and he wanted to graduate from Cottage Grove. We had always attended school there, and I was too intimidated to transfer to E.W. Grove High School in Paris. Fearing that I could not make good grades or maybe even pass, I decided the big city school was not the better option. I also imagined that I would not be able to make new friends or be popular in a different school setting. You see, Grove students were considered snobbish by some of us students at Cottage Grove. They were our great sports rival, and I thought the attending students were out of my social league. Anyway, I had known the kids I went to school with at Cottage Grove since early childhood. I had good friends with whom I felt comfortable; thus, I was confident with my school setting and chose to remain at Cottage Grove School.

After moving from the farmhouse into town, I started attending church in West Paris where our house was located. I met Wanda at church, and she evolved from a casual acquaintance to my new, best friend. Wanda and I were the same age and in the same grade of school. She was a kind of bridge from my past of living in the country to adjusting to city life. We lived in walking distance of each other, so we visited back and forth a lot. I also met David at church. He was the first boy I dated.

After meeting David at church, I discovered that he lived next door. He came to see me not long after we met, and the Tennessee evening was blustery cold with snowflakes falling like crazy. It was a magical night and seemed like a scene from a movie. The two of us engaged in a friendly, flirtatious snowball fight. During our playful encounter, he exclaimed, "All is fair in love and war." That night he asked me for a date (my first actual date). I was euphoric to get to have my first date with such a cute boy who was two years older. From information received from my cousin who attended Grove, David was extremely popular at Grove High School. He played football, was on the student government council, and held numerous other honors. When he graduated, David was selected by classmates to be Mr. Grove. This title was the most valued honor to be attained at Grove in the school's Who's Who selections. My cousin Retta Jane was astonished that her younger cousin would be dating such a popular upper classman. To me, he was just the cute boy next door with dreamy eyes. David was a compassionate, gentle soul, and we shared many kindred thoughts and ideas since his daddy was also an alcoholic. When we talked about what was important to us later in life, we both expressed the strong desire to have a secure, happy home life. We wanted, at all costs, to experience a family life without the turmoil to which we both had been victims due to our daddies' alcohol addictions. After several months of double dating with another couple from church, David and I drifted apart.

When we transitioned from the farm to the house on College Street in Paris, Mother got her GED. She had dropped out of high school to marry my daddy at the young age of fifteen. Having accomplished the GED, she enrolled in LPN school. For about a year and a half, she dedicated herself to getting her LPN degree and license. This woman in her early forties not only graduated but also excelled. Her diligence and determination were rewarded, and she attained second top grades in her class, which included much younger high school graduates. Mother had just begun to tap into her wealth of intelligence and abilities, and I was immensely proud of her accomplishments. Following graduation, she was hired at the Henry County General Hospital in Paris. Mother earned a reputation of possessing not only knowledge but also compassion. Her patients loved her, and there were many requests for her to be the attending nurse.

For most of her adult life, Mother had focused her attention and energies on domestic tasks like tending her babies and children, caring for the house, managing the garden, attending church, participating in the community events, and providing for the school needs of her children. After becoming a nurse, she was thrust into the public workplace surrounded by temptations that had not been present in her life on the farm. She was acknowledged for her performance as a nurse and made friendships with others at the hospital. Her night shifts as a nurse left me unattended in a large rambling house in town. Due to these overnight shifts at the hospital, she gradually stopped attending church. The two of us emerged onto separate roads while we lived on College Street. I clung to my aspirations of achieving my goals of educational excellence and rising above the legacy of an alcoholic daddy. The fact that I was morally and religiously focused provided the foundation I needed to prove I could attain whatever goal I sought. I was determined to accomplish an upright standing and become acknowledged by my peers and others as an honorable, admirable person.

Mother, on the contrary, reacted as if she had been presented a second opportunity of having a thrilling and sensuous life, disregarding, for a season, her moral compass. She began to pursue her own life and dreams, abandoning her parental care of me for a life she had never experienced. Our different paths grew farther apart as time progressed. Independence was the path of choice each of us sought. She pursued her desires as a woman of the world and relinquished her position as my guardian mother. I became an independent woman at fifteen forming decisions void of parental guidance. This early independence could have been detrimental for my character and wellbeing. God's mighty grace protected me by saturating my conscience with a high standard of perfection and morality. I continued my attempt to achieve a righteous standard, because I desired to be viewed by others differently than my daddy had been viewed.

Although my high moral standard was not the way of inward grace as applied to the heart, it was protective grace applied to my outward standards. The outward application of grace enabled me to remain conscientious and morally guarded as a young woman while absent of any hovering paternal guidance or restraints. No one was present to set limits, parameters, or warn me of impending dangers. I praise God that His mighty and wonderful plan included me and that He took care of me during my teenage years.

Following a year of living in Paris and commuting to Cottage Grove School, my cousin Carol, (during an overnight at BeBe's) persuaded me to transfer to Grove High School. In early August before my sophomore school year began, my friend Wanda invited me to attend a Coke party at Grove. The Coke party was staged for the students to claim their previous year's annuals. That party afforded me the opportunity to meet some of the students and eye the date prospects. Well, there was a tall blonde boy that captivated my attention—Richard Vaden. I knew who he was, but I had never met him. One of his cousins and I grew up together, attended the same school, and went to the same church. This cousin had mentioned Richard to some of us girls at Cottage Grove and had shown us pictures of him. I was smitten by Richard's good looks when I saw him that day. During the yearbook event, I did not meet Richard; however, I dreamed of eventually meeting and dating him.

I became good friends with Beth, Richard's cousin, who attended school at Grove. We were in some of the same classes together and developed a fantastic friendship. We shared our boyfriend secrets, and the other secrets teenage girls keep. Beth's mother and daddy, whom I called Aunt Arah and Uncle Duke, were like family to me. They treated me like a daughter and often invited me to their home. After Beth married and left home, Aunt Arah and Uncle Duke's house continued to seem like home to me. Their sweetness and goodness unto me endured while they lived. I shared many confidences with them, and they frequently expressed that they loved me as their own child.

As I attended my new classes at Grove, I sized up all the guys, and none of them interested me. I desired to meet Richard Vaden. Of course, Beth knew that I was infatuated with Richard and began making good comments about me to him. Another twist to the situation was that he and my cousin Retta Jane carpooled about fifteen miles from the country into Paris to attend school. So, I had two different girls campaigning for me regarding Richard. He was a sports enthusiast and played varsity basketball for Grove's Blue Devils. During my sophomore year, I attended one of the season's first games, which was at Springville, Tennessee. That night there was standing room only by the time I arrived, and I was positioned in the doorway to the gym, precariously close to the edge of the basketball court. Both teams charged down the hardwood toward the basketball goal. Richard was propelled to the floor and landed directly in front of me, looking up into my face. Afterwards, he asked my cousin Retta Jane who I was and told her he wanted to meet me. Well, November 20, 1961, Richard called me from Beth's house, and we went on our first date. We doubled dated with his cousin and went to a drive-in movie. Everything went well, and Richard was very respectful to me. I was an incredibly happy young woman, that evening, as Richard walked me to my front door.

We soon had our next date, and Richard asked me to be his steady girl within a couple of weeks. I was ecstatic. I had become the steady girl of one of the most popular boys at Grove High School. How was that possible? I thought I was not on equal footing with him since his daddy was a preacher, and my daddy was a drunk. Nevertheless, I was his steady girlfriend. Richard's daddy was a Baptist preacher at a country church about twelve miles from Paris. On Sunday mornings, church was our date destination. Sunday afternoons consisted of long drives with Richard's cousin and her date, and Sunday nights we were back at church. The four of us spent a lot of time together that first year double dating since Richard was fifteen and did not have his driver's license.

When Richard got his driver's license and a car, we dated more often and were together constantly. During basketball season, varsity games were scheduled on Tuesday and Friday each week. He always picked me up for the hometown games, and he would take me home after the games. He drove me to school every morning, and on weekends he took me to his parents' home to stay overnight. Having me spend the weekends at the Baptist parsonage must have been a difficult situation for his parents to encounter. Nonetheless, Richard insisted that I stay at their house; hence, I was in the parsonage every weekend. My heart sang he cares, he cares. I concluded he wanted to protect me and provide a safe environment for me while having me near.

Being the girl on Richard's arm during high school bolstered my thoughts as to others' acceptance of me. I thought my level of affirmation with the popular kids would increase as his girlfriend because he was one of them. My lack of self-esteem fostered the idea that I needed someone to validate my worthiness. I believed as his girl others would view my worth through him. I was unaware that I did not need anyone to validate me. Throughout my school years at Grove, I endeavored to rise above the perception I thought others had of me. I felt as though others probably considered me as the girl whose daddy was a drunk, the unworthy girl, or the nobody girl. No one ever made any condescending or disdainful remarks to me. My cloak of unworthiness whispered those words of wounded attributes to me, not others. Draped in my cloak of worthlessness, I assumed one had to possess extraordinary qualities or position to be popular and part of the in-crowd at Grove. I hoped my academic achievements would confirm me a position within this crowd. My studious accomplishments boosted my self-image and solidified and affirmed me as part of the in-crowd on my personal merit.

When Richard became part of my life and began crossing boundaries that should have been in place to protect and preserve the very core of whom I was created to be, I interpreted that his actions were prompted by his love for me. The more I succumbed to his control, the more control he exercised. The perception of a person who is chained by a dream or philosophy of love and happiness can misconstrue actions of others due to a clouded view of the facts. We all know well the ancient adage: looking at the world through those rose-colored glasses.

In my mind, the dream of a perfect family centered in God had been manifested in the form of this young man whom I perceived to be a committed Christian. I thought I could not live without Richard Vaden. The evidence of my emotional need of him demonstrated to me a deep love and commitment. I have learned, however, that no one is dependent upon another person to emotionally survive or be happy. In addition, happiness is contingent upon circumstances. Circumstances fluctuate from different levels of wonderful to multiple levels of awful. Consequently, happiness will also fluctuate in varying degrees. Sometimes the feeling of happiness transitions to the far left and is manifested in overwhelming sadness or anger as circumstances evolve. Joy, on the other hand, is the emotion that comes from within when one becomes a child of God. The emotion of joy is evidenced in us by the power of the blessed Holy Spirit. Joy is not contingent upon any circumstance or person, for the source of joy is God. The emotion of desperation does not indicate a healthy and pure emotion of love in a relationship, but rather, it is indicative of a strangling, addictive relationship. Moreover, an individual or the idea of a relationship can be one's drug supply or fix. One can be addicted to a person or relationship like one can be addicted to a substance.

As a young person, I had never read about or been instructed in human behavior or healthy boundaries of love relationships. Foreign to me was the reality of the impediments that arise from dysfunctional personality types within relationships. My interpretation of Richard's actions which exemplified control and manipulation was equated as a demonstration of love. When he told me what to wear or what to do, I translated those actions as a display of his protective care of me. I so urgently desired to please him and to be his girl, that little by little, I released myself to the controlling, manipulative characteristics he epitomized; henceforth, I relinquished bits and pieces of my identity. Most of the letting go of my inner self was a slow, unconscious action on my part, which I did not realize until many years later.

No doubt a definite and undeniable attraction existed between us, as we fervently desired to be with one another. Without intervention or proper guidance, we were left to the ways of our flesh and dysfunction. Neither of us possessed any knowledge of the fundamentals that constituted a grounded, healthy relationship. My insecurities and the overwhelming desire to have the love of a man, this man, were fertile ground for the development of an unhealthy relationship. Contributing to the desire to have the love of a man was the reality that I had experienced in the absence of a healthy bond with my daddy. From birth, a need abides within the heart of a daughter to be loved by her father. When this emotional need is abandoned or not brought to fruition, for whatever reason, the yearning to have the love, affection, and approval of her daddy remains unfulfilled. Sometimes the absence of a godly father and daughter relationship renders the daughter a large hole in the seat of her emotions of love and affection. This gaping hole left in a girl's emotional being continues to exhibit a propensity to be nurtured and causes her to become vulnerable. My state of vulnerability positioned my heart and emotional being in a susceptible condition to be manipulated and controlled.

I mirrored a codependent personality type, while Richard personified the opposite end of the pole with his narcissism. Codependent personalities are natural magnets for the narcissist. Acting as a codependent partner, I constantly sought to meet his needs more than my own needs. My low self-esteem, denial, and compliance unto another were all clinical aspects of the disorder of codependency. Our relationship was paramount unto me, even more important than I was to myself. For our relationship to have functioned in a godly manner, we needed the clear instruction and guidance of the Holy Spirit. For us to have been transformed into viable, nurturing partners, it was fundamental that we embraced the understanding that God needed to be our teacher. A transformation and work completed and manifested by the Holy Spirit was critical but absent.

Richard and I dated throughout high school. We experienced a stormy courtship due to his continuous flirtations and unfaithfulness. Many times, he went behind my back with other girls. He always returned to me, and I always took him back. He and my best friend went on a date one afternoon; feeling guilty, she confessed to me. Otherwise, I guess I would have never known that they had had a rendezvous. Standing on this side of life, I am convinced there were countless encounters with other girls and women that were never known to me. Believe me, I was aware of plenty of his escapades. Sometimes, he secretly made out with other girls during times I was not present. Even more painful were the times that he carried on with someone else in front of me. I just kept taking him back convincing myself that I was the kind of girl he would love and marry. I did not realize as a teenager that I was setting myself up for continued unfaithful behavior from him. By tolerating his pursuit of other girls, while in a relationship with me, sent him the message that he could do as he pleased; I would still be there. Girls need to remember that they are worthy creations of the Father above and deserve respect.

During our senior year, I decided that I would breakup with him as a steady boyfriend. I made sure he knew we were no longer going steady before he went away for a planned weekend visit to his sister's in Memphis. While he was out of town, I was invited to a party with some high school friends. Someone asked to take me home, and I consented. When Richard found out about my date, he was devastated. He told his parents about our breakup and ran off to join the Air Force. His parents were frantic when they contacted me and told me he had run away to join the service. He returned home because he had been too young to join the military without parental consent. It was during our separation that Richard wrote me a letter and expressed how much he loved me. He said that he would always love me, even if we never went back together. In his declaration of love, he wanted me to know if he saw me twenty years later that he would still love me. Eventually, he persuaded me to reconcile with him because he convinced me of his new-found commitment and devotion.

Numerous were the warning signs during our courtship that suggested Richard would not remain faithful. However, I thought as a Christian he had forsaken his wandering eye and ways when I agreed to take him back during our senior year of high school. I was completely in the dark that the other red flags he had unfurled during our high school dating were key elements depicting an overbearing, manipulating, controlling personality of a narcissist. I was ignorant that those terms marked a narcissist (or even the reality of the existence of a narcissist) and void of any ability to identify those attributes in an individual. During the time in high school, he proceeded to exert control over me. One area in which he intruded this power over me was with my clothes. One time, he got upset with me for letting my friend, his cousin, borrow some of my clothes. Richard basically told me what to do and controlled many of my decisions either indirectly or directly. I was flattered as a young woman, since I considered his actions and words were prompted by the emotions of love and care. We continued this tumultuous relationship throughout our high school days.

My journey to advance my image as a respected person and to excel academically was realized during my high school years at E.W. Grove High School. I attended the Top Ten awards banquets two of my three years, was inducted into the National Honor Society in my junior year, held numerous club offices, was appointed Co-Editorship of The Tower (school yearbook), and graduated fifth in my class. I achieved a great rapport with my teachers by demonstrating a conscientious attitude and effort. Upon the recommendation and support of one of my teachers, I applied and was awarded a scholastic scholarship to my college choice. No longer did I have to dream of achieving recognition and respect for I had attained success. Those accomplishments should have been steppingstones to additional achievements, but I was consumed with and focused on my relationship with Richard. He was the single most important person in my life. No, actually, he was the single most important anything in my life.

In addition to contending with the ups and downs of my courtship with Richard, I also struggled with a family loss. My alcoholic daddy died while I was in high school. I was emotionally overcome by his death. Daddy was a young man, about three months' shy of forty-one. He died alone at the house on the farm.

Although he had failed to supply my needs as my father and had not been present for me in a physical, emotional, or spiritual context, I felt I had deserted him in his darkest valley—death. My sense of having deserted him stemmed from the fact that I had not reached out to him while he was alive. Alone in his final hours was the heart-wrenching blow with which I grappled as I faced the reality of his death. The guilt of having not been there for him was an anguishing burden for me. I wrestled repeatedly with the pain of my guilt as it often monopolized my thoughts. I blamed Mother and myself for not being there for him the day he died. It was strange that I accused her since I had previously desired for her to leave him. I had hoped for the peaceful existence we would embrace without him in our lives if she left him. That longing to have peace at home culminated to the point that I had willingly testified of his abuse and alcohol addiction at their divorce trial. Now, I faced his death, and the fact that he was forever gone from our lives.

Days melted into weeks, weeks into months, and gradually the intense guilt subsided to a smaller compartment in my chamber of thoughts. It seemed this devastating event was less painful when I attempted to bury the burden, rather than, expose and confront it. To encounter such calamity head on demanded stability and strength, which at that time in my life I did not possess. Later, the Lord revealed unto me that my strength was in Him not in myself. Eventually, I understood I had not caused the afflictions of James Smyth, had not influenced his lifestyle choices, or had not set-in motion his untimely death. God, by the power of the blessed Holy Spirit, was the only One who could have changed the leper's spots and brought his life to submission by transforming that life into one of obedience.

Richard and I graduated from Grove High School in May 1964, and by October of 1964 we were engaged. We were attending

Murray State College when Richard proposed to me. He proposed to me on the steps of the library, that fall, as we listened to the melody of guitar music. I was overwhelmed with happiness, and I believed my dreams of a love-filled life were unfolding. Believing Richard to be a devoted Christian, I trusted he would be faithful to me after he proposed. With the commitment of engagement and marriage, which he had initiated and embraced, I considered our relationship sealed. I was convinced in my heart that he had ceased his flirtatious ways for he had chosen me. He had made a commitment as a Christian; therefore, I believed he would not stray. My dream of having a loving God-centered family was becoming a reality. Richard had always told me that God told him to marry me. I was persuaded he loved me, and he testified that I was God's choice for him. I chose to believe these were positive reasons to support his commitment to one woman—me.

After becoming engaged, I dropped out of college, and he remained a student. We prepared the upstairs of the house in Paris, where I had lived during high school, to be our apartment following our marriage. We married in a lovely candlelight ceremony in December of 1964 with his daddy officiating. The sanctuary of the beautiful country church, where Richard's daddy was the pastor, was decorated in a festive manner with candles, Christmas ornaments, greenery, and ribbon. My attendants' ensembles were fashioned from red velvet, and they carried bouquets of red flowers mingled with ribbon and ornaments. My wedding gown was stunning with French lace overlaying the fitted bodice. The lace cascaded down the sides of the semi-fitted satin gown, which featured a beautiful chapel length train attached at the waist. My headpiece was a satin double pillbox creation covered lavishly with pearls that showcased an illusion fingertip length veil. I was ecstatic with anticipation and could do nothing but smile. Mother could hardly believe I was not nervous. I was elated because I was marrying the man I loved, who would give me that home for which I had longed since childhood. A home centered in God and His ways.

When my daddy died, I inherited some insurance money; and those were the funds we used to prepare the house, do the wedding, and, of course, buy a new car. We remained in the upstairs of the house for about one month. Friends of ours bought a mobile home, and we decided to purchase a mobile home also. Again, we used my inheritance to buy the mobile home.

The first place we parked the trailer was in Paris, Tennessee. We lived there for a few months, and I worked at a local television parts factory after I discontinued college. Not long after Richard finished his first semester, we moved the mobile home to Memphis. He sought employment in retail at Sears in the tire and automotive department. I managed to secure a job at a Federal Reserve Bank and was training for my position when he was fired from his job at Sears. He unknowingly violated the rules regarding selling on a percentage type incentive. We decided to move the trailer near our home of Paris. So, our mobile home was indeed very mobile with three moves in a few short months.

We rented a lot on the highway between Paris, Tennessee, and Murray, Kentucky, and we parked our mobile home there. Our trailer was in the little town of Puryear, Tennessee, about ten miles from his mother and daddy's parsonage. Richard got a job in the warehouse division at Emerson Electric manufacturing plant in Paris. I did not work that summer, but I spent a lot of time at Richard's grandmother's house who lived in Puryear. The two of us developed a strong bond that summer. Neighbors and family members shared their garden bounty with her, and I would go to her house to help her preserve the food. She taught me how to can vegetables, and we canned several quarts of green beans. We sat on the front porch to snap the beans and prepare them to can in her water bath canner. While we waited for them to process for two hours, we visited as we completed other chores. Another garden treat we canned was a homemade tomato relish she called chili sauce. It took hours to prepare and can, but it was a recipe of hers that I kept and treasured over the years. I loved Mammy Ruth's fellowship and enjoyed learning how to can. It was a special opportunity, and we grew close that summer as she mentored me.

After working in the warehouse position for the summer, Richard decided to return to college at Murray State. We moved our mobile home to a lot in Murray, Kentucky, not far from the college. Richard enrolled in college that fall, and I worked in a Ben Franklin's Five and Dime Store. Our ideas of his expectations in school were not on the same page. I thought it should be his job. I anticipated that he should do well or at the very least attend class. Well, sometimes, he had guys over at night to play cards. After a late night of card playing, he did not always make it to his early class the next morning. I expressed my dislike and anger at his behavior as well as his lack of effort in school. One night when he and his friends were playing cards, I awoke in the middle of the night to find them still there. I got up, went into the kitchen, and opened and slammed all the cabinet doors. I never said a word, but everyone got the message and left. I was so angry. He was living the life of a college bum while I supported us. I did not intend to continue down that path. Working hard did not bother me, but I expected him to do his part. Richard barely scraped by in college that semester. Since his college effort was not productive, he did not enroll for the next semester and began pursuing an enlistment in the Air Force. The previous semester had ended in late December and by the first week of March, he left for basic training in the Air Force.

While we lived in the mobile home in Murray, Kentucky, mother remarried for a brief period and my half-sister was born. My contact with my sister Gina was limited since she was born after I had married. It was not long after her birth that Richard and I moved across the continental United States. Our lives from that point seemed to be in different worlds; thus, Gina and I did not have a functioning relationship as sisters. While Mother was alive, I visited with my sister a few times over the years. The last time I saw Gina was at our brother's funeral. We did not stay in contact; therefore, my attempts to locate her have been futile.

Following Richard's enlistment in the Air Force, we sold the mobile home. I lived with his mother and daddy until he finished his training. My job situation improved as I secured a job at the Murray-Calloway County Hospital in the pharmacy. I also operated the storeroom for the hospital. I worked diligently to organize and restructure the hospital storeroom and compiled a new catalog for all the supplies and materials. I was the individual to whom requisitions were submitted for needed medical items throughout the hospital. I enjoyed my job and excelled in the organizational capacity. I did not realize, at that time, that the ability to structure, detail, and organize were strengths with which I had been gifted. I was praised for my accomplishments, but due to a move dictated by Richard's military enlistment, my position was short lived.

Military Days, Return Home, and Corporate Journey

By the time Richard entered the Air Force, he had bought the third car. This time he ordered a convertible. Each time he bought a car I would get extremely upset, but I never stopped him. I allowed him to spend the money, although I did not agree with the spending. Before we married, I had gone before a judge to have my age disabilities removed, so I could access my inheritance from my daddy to go to college. The judge made a profound statement to me that day. He said, "Now do not let some young man take your money and buy a car." Wow, oh, wow! I did not follow his advice or realize the truth of his prophetic words. No, I magnified his prophecy. He certainly was a wise man and knew how a young woman could fall prey to the whims of the man she loved. If young people would only heed the wisdom of their elders, many pitfalls and mistakes could be avoided. Oh, but I was so in love.

After Richard enlisted in the Air Force and went away for basic training, we wrote each other daily. His mother and daddy took me to visit him while he was in basic training at Lackland Air Force Base in Texas, and he got a weekend pass for married guys. As soon as he finished basic at the Air Force base in San Antonio, he was transferred for his technical training to a base just outside Amarillo. When Richard was given clearance to live off the base in Amarillo on weekends, we decided I would move to Texas. I packed the car with necessary household items and my little wirehair fox terrier doggy. I journeyed from his parents' rural home near Paris, Tennessee, to spend the night in Memphis at his sister's house. I arose in the wee hours of the morning and embarked to new horizons of flat lands, gusty winds, and big sky—Texas.

Excited as a word of portrayal of what I felt certainly failed to embrace the fullness in my heart that day. I had never been on a road trip alone, well, almost alone; I had my doggie, you remember. Little Princess was my partner in crime, and we made it fine to our destination. I spent my first night on the road somewhere in Texas. The new scenery was such a contrast to my native home in beautiful West Tennessee. My road trip was exhilarating and adventurous as I discovered the captivating landscapes of the open, vast land of Texas. My heart and dreams were somewhere floating in the clouds as I contemplated, with breathtaking anticipation, the reality of reuniting with Richard. I was on an emotional high throughout my journey.

After I arrived at my destination in Amarillo, I rented a basic furnished apartment, which was located close to the Air Force base. Richard stayed with me at the apartment on weekends, and we were euphoric to be together. During the weeknights while I was alone in the apartment, I heard people partying in the adjoining apartments, and I was terrified. I feared that someone would notice that I was alone throughout the week and take advantage of me. With my dog, Princess, perched upon the bed with me, I read each night until I exhausted into sleep. I also kept a small, loaded handgun on the night table beside the bed. Having a loaded gun was potentially dangerous because I doubt, I could have managed to use it safely in my defense.

Richard's technical school was delayed. While we were waiting for his school to commence, he was approved for military leave, and we traveled to Tennessee for a visit. We picked up the new convertible while we were at home. When we returned to Texas, we moved from our location in Amarillo to Canyon, Texas. We relocated to apartments where several other young military couples resided. The husbands of these couples were all attending various technical schools. The guys carpooled back and forth to the base, and the wives hung out with each other and stayed pool side much of the time.

After tech school was completed, Richard got his permanent duty assignment to George Air Force Base in the Mojave Dessert. When I heard Mojave Desert, all I could picture in my mind were sand dunes and women with veils over their faces. I said, "Where is the Mojave Desert, and can I go with you?" Of course, it was state side in beautiful, sunny Southern California. Great excitement followed the news of our assignment to California. This Tennessee country girl had moved up. First, I had traveled to Texas, home of the Alamo, and now, I would be headed to the home of Hollywood in Southern California. New horizons were ahead to see and conqueror.

We had our convertible for only a short time. When others heard that we would be stationed in the dessert, they advised us to sell the convertible. The basis for their advice was that the top would be destroyed in the sun and sand of the Mojave Desert. While on leave in Tennessee after tech school and prior to our move to California, Richard headed to the car dealership to trade the new convertible. It was car number four in about a year and a half. That time not only did he trade our car, but he also traded our ski boat and motor. We drove away from the dealership in a bright blue, new Impala. After our month's leave following basic and technical school, we headed to our first base assignment at George Air Force in sunny Southern California.

Shortly after arriving and settling into our apartment in Apple Valley, California, Richard had to report to the Air Force base to complete a required desert training program, which lasted several days. While he was gone for the training, I became ill with extreme nausea and vomiting. The young woman who lived in the apartment next door was my caregiver. She supplied me Seven Up and Payday candy bars to keep me going. That was the only sustenance I wanted and could eat. We had no air conditioning in the apartment, and the warm apartment made the nausea and vomiting worse. Richard rushed me to the base emergency room when he returned from the desert training. The doctor, who checked me, told me my illness would last about nine months. I was pregnant, and my heart was jubilant. I was going to be a mother! My pregnancy went well, and I followed the protocol of the military doctor and his staff. I did not gain much weight during pregnancy, so my pregnant belly was the only obvious sign. While pregnant, we went with some friends and their parents to Disney World in California. Richard would not walk beside me at Disney World, because I was pregnant. My friend's mother was appalled by the way he treated me, and my feelings were crushed by his actions.

Our firstborn arrived March 27, 1967, at the hospital on George Air Force Base located in the Mojave Desert of Southern California. My attending nurse (an Air Force officer), during my labor, was an older white-haired woman. I was convinced she had never birthed children, because her compassion toward me was way, way down the scale in the minus column. She told me cats birthed their kittens and cleaned up the mess. Thankfully, I had been blessed with a kind doctor. I was in labor about six hours and did not receive anything for pain until I was taken into the delivery room. I was administered a saddle block as the baby was crowning. I thought next time I might attempt birthing my baby without any anesthetic. John Allen Vaden weighed 7 pounds and 11 ounces and had a scant swatch of blonde hair; hence, I called him my cotton top. He resembled a little old man because his hair was so blonde that he appeared bald. My first born was beautiful to me, and I could not do anything but smile after his birth. He prospered and became a chubby little boy by the time he turned three months. I loved and doted on my little boy and was in awe of each new trick and milestone he conquered.

When John was around one year old, we moved from the Mojave Desert in Southern California to San Bernardino, California, about an hour away. I had decided to enroll in a medical assisting class, and the school was in San Bernardino. Some of our Air Force friends lived next door to the apartment we rented, and the wife watched our little John while I went to school. Several airmen who were stationed at George Air Force Base with Richard lived in San Bernardino, and the guys carpooled to the base. The desert town of Victorville, which was close to George Air Force Base, was small and did not offer any exciting attractions for young people, so many of the airman moved to the big city of San Bernardino. The base was surrounded by vast expanses of forsaken desert, Joshua trees, and rock mountains. George Air Force Base was a training base for pilots, and the open desert spaces provided an appropriate landscape for their training. The only place of interest I heard about in the desert area was the ranch of the famed Roy Rogers and Dale Evans in nearby Apple Valley. This was also the location of our first apartment. The lure of San Bernardino and nearby Big Bear Mountains, therefore, beckoned the young airmen and their families away from the desolate desert. If the snowy mountains did not captivate your attention, maybe some of the nearby fabulous beaches of Southern California would. About an hour from San Bernardino in one direction took you to the snow of the Big Bear Mountains, and an about an hour in a different direction took you to the beautiful Pacific Ocean and sandy beaches.

I enjoyed school and worked hard to excel. When graduation arrived a year and half later, I had achieved the top grades and earned the distinction of giving the awards speech at the ceremony. Richard went to a bowling tournament that evening instead of going with me to support my accomplishments. I was so hurt that I did not have anyone standing in my corner rooting for me, especially Richard. Later, the owner of the school told me that her adult son had come for the graduation festivities and had fallen in love with me. My secret admirer, who remained a secret to me, was a mental and emotional encouragement.

The girl with the second-ranked grades and I with the top honors were awarded internships at the office of the top Obstetrician/Gynecologist in San Bernardino. The internship, which was required by the school, was the final month of our school and training. By the end of the internship, I had captured the attention of the doctor and his office manager because I was more mature than the other candidate and exemplified a diligent work ethic. I was chosen as the medical assistant for his office and was employed for two years prior to Richard's discharge from the Air Force.

It was confirmed before departing California that I was pregnant with our second child. I experienced an episode of bleeding just before we were to journey back to Tennessee. My doctor advised me not to drive the long distance from California to our home in Tennessee, as he thought it could initiate additional problems and concerns for the new pregnancy. We decided I would travel home by plane instead of the car. Little John and I boarded a flight bound for Memphis, Tennessee, and Richard drove the journey home, alone.

During a stop on his drive back to Tennessee, he committed infidelity. He stopped to visit with close friends we had made while in the Air Force. The wife was visiting with her parents while she was awaiting the arrival of her husband from deployment. Richard arrived at the parent's home the night before the husband was scheduled to be there. One would think the wife would be eagerly anticipating her husband's imminent arrival and reunion. Richard and she, however, acted on lustful desires committing their betrayal in her parents' home after the parents retired to bed. It was years later before Richard disclosed this indiscretion to me.

The friendship with the couple continued for a few years. Our husbands eventually had the same employer, after they were discharged from the Air Force. We visited with the couple while I remained in total darkness as to what had transpired that night at her parents' home. Richard betrayed me and he deceived me by withholding the knowledge of his actions. It was in this deceptive atmosphere that we continued a relationship with this couple. I later realized his actions with this woman was only one adulterous incident that he had concealed during our marriage. Throughout our marriage, Richard always maintained that he had never been unfaithful to me, because he said he had never had sex with anyone but me. His definition regarding adultery and sex were on the opposite end of the spectrum from the views that I held and hold. He held the viewpoint that anything short of sexual relations was not adultery, nor was it considered sexual. I believed and continue to maintain that when one of the married partners goes outside of the marriage and participates in any lustful act, whether mental, verbal, or physical; he has committed adultery.

Oblivious to his unfaithfulness, life continued in a normal pattern. We were delighted to be home in Tennessee after being away four years with his Air Force enlistment. Richard took the appropriate tests and applied for a job at the post office. As a veteran, he was given an advantage over other applicants and secured a position with the post office. We were excited about him working at the post office, which paid well and offered great benefits. With my medical assistant's education and practical work experience, I managed to appropriate a job at one of the prominent clinics in our hometown. I was hired to cover for the nurse of the founder of the clinic. Both of us were pregnant, but she was due to deliver much sooner than I. Funny, a pregnant woman was hired to take over for another pregnant woman. The clinic had previously made plans to add a pediatrician to the staff, and I was promised the position as his nurse.

Before our baby arrived, we built a three-bedroom home midway between Richard's parents' rural parsonage and our workplaces in town. The home site we chose was close to friends. They had built a house in the same subdivision earlier and recommended their contractor. Since the location of the lot was in a rural area, we secured a reasonable loan payment and interest rate established to benefit rural property applicants. The small rural town boasted a post office, a few churches, a school, barber and beauty shops, a diner or two, a grocery, and gas stations. I am sure the quaint, little town had additional businesses which I have forgotten over the passage of a half of a century. On the outskirts of the town, a country club was built, and we joined the membership.

My heart was extremely happy during those days. I was married to my high school sweetheart, was a mother to a three-year old son, and was moving into a new house. Talk about hopes and dreams coming true; I was on top of the world. We lived with Richard's parents for three months while our house was built. His mother bought the fabric and assisted me in fashioning all the window treatments for the new house. She was the scissor lady and cut the fabric for the curtains and drapes. I kept the sewing machine humming as I crafted the fabric into curtains. We were a tremendous team as we made all those window coverings. She worked fast, and I could pull the fabric through the sewing machine as quickly as she funneled it to me. Before our new little bundle of love arrived, the curtains were finished, and each window in that adorable little house had charming window treatments.

The exterior façade of our house was a deep red brick with a dark charcoal, almost black, mortar filling the brick joints. The front design of the house featured a moderate size front porch and an attached enclosed garage. I had chosen greens, blues, and soft yellowy golds for my color scheme. Green (avocado) appliances, which were a rage in the late sixties and seventies, were a definite must have. The kitchen featured a built-in stove top and oven, which in 1970, made me feel like we owned a designer home. The counter tops of the lovely, stained cabinets were pricey matte-finished ceramic tile. Our contractor offered us the counter tops at a discounted price in exchange for our kitchen functioning as a showroom. I was thrilled that I could choose the trendy shag style carpet, which we purchased from a local discount carpet outlet.

We moved our furnishings, which had been in storage since our departure from the Air Force to our new address. My excitement was off the charts as I unpacked, arranged furniture, and put the final touches on our home. I had painted furniture for the children's bedrooms and decorated them to reflect each of the children. Although the baby had not been born, I was convinced that I was having a baby girl and decorated accordingly. We purchased some new pieces of furniture for our family room, which was part of the open space with the kitchen and dining area. It was like a doll house and reflected my style implicitly. Since I was a highly motivated and driven personality type, I achieved my goal of organizing and completing my interior design efforts in time to welcome my precious baby girl to our cozy, stylish new house.

How could life be any better? I had my man, a gorgeous little boy, a beautiful baby girl, a new house, and attended church where Richard's daddy was the pastor. We both had great jobs and were experiencing this wonder and excitement close to family and friends. The dreams I had envisioned were being fulfilled. I did have one disappointment after Amy was born. I did not want to leave her and John to return to work. I went back to my job in only two weeks following her birth and cried every single day. Her great grandmother, Mammy Ruth, came every day to the house to take care of her. The people that operated the daycare where John stayed were well known by Richard's mother and daddy, so I felt they were trustworthy.

I did not worry at all about my baby girl receiving good care and love. Mammy Ruth loved Amy as if she were her own baby. She told me caring for Amy was like getting to have her two babies who had died while they were infants. Amy was a joy to Mammy Ruth, and Mammy Ruth was a precious gift unto Amy. Amy would tell her grandmother, "I love you MeMa, but I really love Mammy Ruth." It was okay for the two of them to be so connected. We all acknowledged that they had a bond. It was not a matter of Amy being loved while I was at work, but, rather, it was a matter of someone else caring for my baby and my little boy instead of me. I wanted to stay home and take care of my children, for that was where my heart abided. My heart was not career minded. I wanted to fully embrace the roles of wife, mother, and homemaker.

Although our lives seemed picture perfect during the time we settled in our new home with our son and new baby girl, Richard's anger surfaced with a vengeance of which I had not realized he was capable. I purchased a pant dress, a fashion trend at the time, and he detested it. He had warned me if he saw me wearing it again, he would take it off me. Guess I did not take him seriously, and I also was more independent minded at that time. Anyway, I was wearing the dress one day when he, unexpectedly, came home. He went into a rage and started ripping off the dress. Well, I never wore the dress again because he destroyed it. Another time, while we lived in our new house, he became violent and shoved my head through the sheet rock wall in the laundry room. I was both terrified and embarrassed that he would do something so horrific and dangerous to me. I buried his violent actions in my mind, and I never spoke to anyone of his abuse to me. I felt too embarrassed to admit to anyone that the man, with whom I had chosen to spend my life, would hurt me. I loved him, and he loved me; therefore, I reasoned that he would not hurt me again. I certainly was not planning on leaving this man I loved. Things would surely be better, and this type of behavior from him would never happen again.

I protected Richard and subjected myself to the probability of additional trauma by never telling anyone that he had abused me. I did not tell law enforcement, family, or even a friend. I concealed my pain and continued as if he had done nothing. He would say he was sorry but in such a way that I had to assume the blame for whatever he had done. What he did to me in his anger was, by his standard, ultimately, my fault. I became an accomplice in his abuse toward me. Whether the abuse was physical, emotional, or verbal, I took on the blame and stayed *silent*. I enabled Richard to continue such actions unto me because he realized I was not going to rat on him or leave him. Apart from Richard's sudden outbursts of anger and abuse, life was busy and mostly ordinary. I was unaware that I was setting the stage for continued abuse throughout my marriage to him. I set him upon a pedestal and began the journey of protection for him and deceit unto myself. I had entered a world clouded with fantasy.

Richard continued his pursuit of a college degree and commuted to college after he finished his workday at the post office. As I drove home from work each night, we would pass each other on the highway as he headed to college. Years later, he confessed unto me that he had encountered flirtatious interactions with females, especially one girl, while a student at the college. On the other hand, my routine, when I returned home from work in the evenings, was caring for my children, tending to the house, and sewing. Richard's mother kept me supplied with tons of fabric from the business where she worked. Amy had a multitude of precious little dresses and creations, that I fashioned. It was such fun to sew for my little princess. I made all my clothes using mostly McCall patterns and fabric that MeMa gave me. I loved being a mother, and I enjoyed performing household tasks. My heart was happiest when I performed in my roles of wife, mother, and homemaker.

We attended the Baptist church where Richard's daddy preached, and we were present on Sunday mornings, Sunday nights, and Wednesday night prayer meetings. During childhood, I attended a Baptist church in my community, and I made a profession of salvation when I was nine years old. My profession was at the same time many of the children in the church professed salvation. I had wanted to do the right thing but had not understood you needed to be drawn by the Holy Spirit. My profession had been a movement of the flesh to do right. Not long after my profession, my Sunday school teacher began teaching about repentance regarding salvation. It troubled me because I realized I had not experienced repentance. As a teenager, I became increasingly sensitive to the work of the Holy Spirit. My heart was awakened, and I was under compelling conviction that I needed Jesus as my Savior. After I married and had John and Amy, I continued to experience a work of the Holy Spirit and wrestled with conviction. One Sunday during a revival, the visiting preacher propounded from the book of Daniel about the incident when the fingers of a man's hand appeared and wrote on the wall of King Belshazzar's palace. Daniel was called to interrupt the writing on the wall. One thing Daniel related to the king was that one could be weighed on the balances (scales) and could be found lacking. My heart was pierced with the arrow of the Holy Spirit, and I knew there was no place to run and hide any longer for He had stripped me of my mask. My good morals, my reformation, and self-deeds would not suffice, for I needed Jesus. I confessed and received Jesus as my Savior. No more did I look to myself or good morals, for I had a Savior, my all in all.

We had lived in our precious house a little over one year when some of our Air Force friends reconnected with us. He persuaded Richard to put college on hold and apply for a position in the company where he had worked since leaving the Air Force. The appeal of working for a huge corporation and getting to relocate had an attraction for both of us. Richard envisioned climbing the corporate ladder, and I dreamed of being a stay-at-home mother. He traveled to meet and interview with the company representative and was hired. He gave his resignation to the postal service, and I resigned my job at the clinic. We sold the adorable little house we had built. His parents were startled, hurt, and confused. They thought we had come home to raise our family. After all, we had dependable jobs and a new home. We were young, impulsive, ready for adventure, and succumbed to the lure of making money, while anticipating the excitement the corporate world had to offer. How could we possibly leave our great jobs and our family? We were very eager to chase the dream and make our mark in the corporate world. I was confident that we would succeed. After selling our home, Richard temporarily relocated to accomplish the training for his new job with Levi Strauss. The children and I went to his mother and daddy's home to live and waited for his designated assignment. Richard did some of his training for the new position in Albuquerque, New Mexico, and I flew there to be with him for a weekend. We were on our corporate journey.

The friend from the Air Force that had influenced Richard to join the ranks of the corporate world was the same one whose wife had committed infidelity with Richard. They had gotten together on the eve of her husband's return from deployment. At that time, I had no idea I was befriending the *other woman*. We had been friends for a few years, and I certainly was not aware such a betrayal had taken place. We continued our friendship while our husbands were employed by the same company. Our paths frequently crossed, and we visited in each other's homes. We traveled together when our husbands' jobs had coinciding business destinations. I remained unaware and unsuspecting of Richard's dark secret.

The first position assigned to Richard with Levi was in quality control at a manufacturing plant in Valdosta, Georgia. We loaded up, with John and Amy in tow, for what I imagined would be a vacation while we looked for a suitable house. You know, we would have hotel accommodations with meals provided. I had envisioned that this adventure of finding our house would be such fun. How wrong I was. Traveling, living out of suitcases, and staying in a motel with two young children while house hunting was not a vacation. We managed to find a house I loved in an established neighborhood, which featured a beautiful yard. The house had a playhouse in the back yard for John and Amy, making it perfect. The yard was well-manicured and had huge pine trees in both the front and back yards. We purchased the house and had new carpet installed. I had to perform a deep cleaning on the house before I unpacked. I was so intrigued exploring the features of the home that I failed to notice how desperately it needed cleaning. I wept while I cleaned, because a mountain of boxes waited to be unpacked by me alone. I kept focused and managed to get the house spic and span clean, organized, and decorated in record time.

As a lot of young people do, we stretched the budget to make the house situation work. I had not planned to get a job after Richard went to work for Levi Strauss. I had wanted to realize my dream to be a stay-at-home mom. Richard applied the pressure for me to look for work. I went on a job search and secured a position in a periodontal surgeon's office. When Richard came home the night following my first day at work and found no supper on the table, my position in the periodontal office came to a screeching halt. He deemed himself more important than coming in second to me working. Of course, I was relieved, as I never wanted to be in the public work environment anyway.

Not many months into his new position with Levi in Georgia, everything at home and between us changed. At the onset of the change, I did not understand what had happened. When Richard withdrew from all intimate contact between us, I realized what was transpiring. It was not too difficult from that point to figure out that he was having an affair. He camouflaged the whole scenario to confuse me as to who the *other woman* was. He acted as if she were someone at the conservative church we attended. Roadblocks were thrown all along the way to deflect whatever suspicions I had of who she was. During his affair, he asked me if I thought he should check on his secretary who was in the hospital with a heart problem. I told him I thought that would be a good idea, not realizing she was the woman with whom he was having the affair.

Mother became critically ill while Richard was indulging in his adulterous behavior. My sister who lived in South Carolina and I (along with John and Amy) drove to Kentucky together to see about Mother. Stress and anxiety concerning Richard's behavior during my absence flooded my mind and distracted me from tending to Mother. I imagined all kind of scenarios transpiring with the *other woman*. My level of trepidation was so staggering that I pleaded with my sister to culminate the trip and return to Georgia. I did not disclose my reasons for my sudden, pressing need to prematurely journey home. I cannot recall what imaginary roadblock I used to camouflage my actual reasons for my urgency. My suspicions were pretty much spot on because he and the *other woman* had a rendezvous while I was in Kentucky. The details of their affair were unknown to me except the occasional bits and pieces Richard divulged. He asked me if I had noticed a certain car passing by our house because the woman's husband had threatened him. Another time, I suspected that Richard had taken little Amy to a shopping mall to meet the woman. He later confirmed my suspicion. He asked if he divorced me, would I demand custody of both John and Amy. I told him he could have whatever he wanted of the household items, but he was not getting my children. The remainder of our time in Valdosta was a struggle of emotional turmoil. My heart was shattered, and my world was turned upside down. I was consumed with the brokenness of my marriage and turned unto God to sustain me.

Amid the tumult and uncertainty of our marital distress, Richard continued to perform well with his work. He was productive at Levi and was soon promoted. His new assignment would relocate us to Corinth, Mississippi, and this relocation was scheduled to take place prior to Christmas. Richard told me that he was attending the Levi plant Christmas party before we left Valdosta for our relocation to Corinth, whether I liked it or not. His attitude about attending the party confirmed to me that it was to be with his secretary. He went to the party, and I was hurt and angry. Although our marriage seemed hopeless, we made the move together for him to take the new position in Corinth.

Through all the conflict and depression surrounding the affair, I lost about twenty pounds. I prayed for our marriage and begged Richard to stay. It was a dark valley and deep pit that had devoured me in my young Christian life. I was determined to not let Satan have the victory. It was a paradoxical situation because I did not want to lose this adulterer, this abuser. I clung to this man and marriage, although he was the basis for my broken heart and grief. Why could I not let him go? Why did I insist on holding on to someone who obviously did not want to be with me? In addition to my relentless determination to not let go was my perception that divorce was wrong. I was convinced that God wanted me to fight for my marriage. While I was in my dark valley and the deep miry pit during that fragile time, God was with me. What seemed utter destruction and despair yielded in me the peaceable fruit of righteousness. If you are downtrodden under the heavy load of care, look up for your help resides in God your Father, not people.

God is our refuge and strength, a very present help in trouble (Psalm 46:1 KJV).

Seek Him and ask Him to open your eyes to His way and His wisdom. It is difficult to separate our flesh from our spirit and to be able to discern the difference. Oh, the war we encounter between the flesh and the spirit. The rulers of darkness would have one to believe a lie; furthermore, Satan is seeking the people of God to destroy or render crippled as they endeavor to finish their earthly journey. He whispered defeat and mocked me when I called on God. The powers of darkness said, "if God loved you, why did He let this happen?" I was taunted for casting my care upon my heavenly Father. What lie has been whispered in your ear by the great deceiver? My heart was ravaged because of Richard's affair. Doubt and fear assailed me. I was so thankful and eager to leave Valdosta, but my trust in Richard was destroyed. From that time of unfaithfulness by him, I struggled to believe he was not going to repeat the same scenario with someone else. As I experienced the weakness of my flesh, I desired to evade and flee the scene of the battlefield of indiscretions and deception I had encountered in Georgia.

The relocation to Corinth, Mississippi, transpired in time for us to go home and spend Christmas with family. Our home in Paris was a two-hour drive from Corinth. We rented a nice, large house before embarking on our visit home. After Christmas, Richard's parents came and helped us paint the interior of the house we had rented. I unpacked, after all the painting and cleaning was finished, and a new chapter in our lives began to unfold. One area of our lives that needed adjustment following our move was our son's kindergarten. The move to Mississippi had disrupted John's school year. Since we had relocated in the middle of the school year, we were unable to find a kindergarten with an opening to enroll him. I became his instructor, so he could finish his kindergarten school year. According to John, I was a hard teacher.

Another area of our life that we had to deal with after our move was the remnants of Richard's affair. The wounds to my heart were not healed, and my distrust continued to be an issue. Richard traveled a lot for his job and had to return, on occasion, to Valdosta where we had lived during his unfaithfulness. Confronting my fears of distrust when he returned to that place was extremely difficult. I believe my heartache and distrust would have been less difficult to overcome had Richard openly confessed and sought my forgiveness. He did not come forward with a contrite heart and seek to make amends; instead, he chose to not mention the breach between us. The only time we ever talked about the affair was when I would, in desperation, say something. Richard remained defensive and continued in denial concerning the depth of his betrayal or the extent of my wounds. He preferred to act as if his entire transgression were nonexistent. I could not change him or the situation, so I sought the Lord for help. Life just continued.

We prayed and searched for a church to attend in our new location. While listening to a local radio station, we were drawn to the host of the morning show. His love for the Lord was apparent, and we investigated to identify the church he attended. We located the church and decided this was the church the Lord would have us visit. The church was without a pastor, but we were certain this was where God wanted us to serve Him. An immediate connection with the radio announcer and his wife transpired, and they became our new, best buddies. They befriended us and took us under their wings. As the people of the church searched for a new pastor, we joined them in the search. Soon a fiery fortyish-aged preacher was called to fill the vacated pastor position, and we loved and supported him. Many new friendships were formed within the church, and our hearts felt we had found home.

After living only six months in the Corinth location, Levi Strauss offered Richard a divisional position. This was quite a leap from his beginning job and was an impressive promotion in a short time. Now, we had advanced up several rungs of that corporate ladder. His new position would relocate us to East Tennessee close to the beautiful Smokey Mountains. His office location would be in Knoxville, so we traveled there in search for a house. Our house search lasted for a few days, and we stayed with a cousin of Richard's and her family. The area of our house search was in Maryville, which was a suburb of Knoxville. Our selection of houses was vast, but we narrowed it down to one house. We were on the verge of signing a contract; however, we elected to go get a coke and talk it over. It was our decision that we would head back to Corinth, pray about the house, and call the real estate agent to give her an answer after spending the weekend at home.

A New Path

Our church conducted a tent revival that began the weekend we returned to Corinth from Knoxville. During the attendance of this revival, Richard wrestled with the idea that God had called him to preach. He and our radio announcer friend drove a couple of hours to see Richard's daddy to have prayer regarding his call to preach. He surrendered to preach that day in his daddy's living room. With his surrender to preach the gospel, my heart had a renewed hope that our marriage would endure. I reasoned that a preacher would change and be faithful to his marriage.

Richard submitted a two-week notice to his boss at Levi, and our lives took a dramatic turn. He enrolled in a Southern Baptist Bible college in Blue Mountain, Mississippi, and I went to work. One of the deacons of Oakland Baptist Church, where we attended, owned a hosiery mill. I was given a prime position in production at the plant. He hired me to work in the same capacity as his daughters-in-law as an inspector. I was diligent at the hosiery mill and was paid by a production scale. I watched the clock and calculated how many pantyhose I needed to inspect each hour to make or excel production. Some of the other employees walked around and joked with others during the workday. The only reason I was there was to provide a living for my family, so I worked fast and furious to make as much as possible. Another deacon of our church owned a construction business. He provided a new house for us to enjoy, completely free of charge, for the remainder of our residence in Corinth. Since the house was at the construction stage to choose the interior décor, the generous deacon/contractor gave me the fun privilege of making all the design choices.

Our good friends the radio announcer and his wife supported us in many ways. Each morning on the way to work, I dropped John at their house, so he could ride the bus to school. After dropping John at their house each morning, I took my little princess to her babysitter. They also helped with the children whenever there was a need, and their teenage daughter babysat for us sometimes in the evenings or for special occasions. Everyone at Oakland Baptist Church adored our children, John and Amy. Many of the sweet people in the church reached out to help us during this time of transition. While my employment at the hosiery plant was our supporting income, Richard received his GI bill that covered his college expenses.

During the time we lived in Corinth and served at Oakland Baptist Church, I formed a close friendship with a precious lady. Although she was older than I, we became friends due to our shared love of the Lord. Our spiritual kinship in the Lord drew us together in shared times of prayer and fellowship. The two of us met each week before the Wednesday church service to pray together. We had a desire to follow Christ and grow in Him, and our bond continued for many years until her tragic death. We eventually moved from Corinth, but she and I stayed in contact. In the last years of her life, she lived close to us.

Before Richard completed the credits for his degree, he was called to pastor Southside Baptist Church, which was located about two hours south of Corinth. After accepting the call to pastor the church in Aberdeen, we moved to the parsonage. The house had three bedrooms, two baths, and a large open space in the front of the house that functioned as the formal living room with adjoining dining room. A spacious family room and kitchen with dining area was in the back portion of the house. The parsonage was located on a plot of land behind the church building, and I enjoyed making the roomy house our home. Decorating was a fun opportunity to create a space which reflected my tastes and make the house feel like home to the children. We settled in and started our new life as pastor and pastor's wife. John was enrolled in the elementary school and played baseball in the summer. Soon, Amy attended kindergarten at the First Baptist Church and made best friends with a member's little girl in our new church. Richard continued to pursue his college after becoming the pastor of Southside and graduated with a Bachelor of Arts from the Southern Baptist college in Blue Mountain, Mississippi.

Although deeply distraught by his unfaithful behavior with his secretary at Levi Strauss Manufacturing, I forgave him. I had reaffirmed hope that he had repented in his heart and had begun to be faithful to me; although, Richard never asked my forgiveness. I trusted, as a man of God, he had cleaned up his act and would portray a godly lifestyle. Nevertheless, I was aware that he continued to possess a tendency to spend time with other females. Sometimes this included flirtations or involved conversations. My trust of him was tarnished, and smoking guns surfaced in his journey as a young preacher man. Women pursued him, and he seemed reluctant to discourage their attraction unto him. His previous unfaithfulness, accompanied by my lack of self-esteem, affected my trust of him; I was suspicious of his encounters with other females. If I approached him about any questionable behavior, he would become defiant. He denied any wrong, telling me I was overly jealous. He was defensive and stated that I had imagined the entire situation.

Southside multiplied in attendance rapidly, and before long, Richard led the church in a building program. Initially, some of the founding fathers resisted the building program, but they came on board once they realized it was going forward with or without them.

Plans for a large auditorium and offices were made, and construction began. Richard stayed extremely busy finishing his degree, leading the building program, and performing the many pastoral duties. As the new pastor in the local Baptist association, he was invited to preach revivals in several churches in the outlying areas of the county. He was the area's most sought after preacher, and in this quaint Southern town, he was also the most talked about pastor.

Richard devoted extraordinary amounts of time to the church people and their problems, rarely affording windows of time for our children or me. The positions of a pastor and the wife of a pastor of a Southern Baptist church were demanding positions. Every waking moment seemed to have been consumed by the needs and whims of the congregation or their extended families. The pastoral duties extended to oversee the spiritual scope and financial structure of the church. As pastor of a Southern Baptist church, Richard had to function much like the CEO of a business, except he dealt with matters of the heart, mind, and spirit instead of black and white guidelines in a handbook printed and controlled by the business. This enormous responsibility required seemingly endless time and effort.

I felt alone a greater portion of the time in my new position for I had no close friend or confidant. During the experience as a pastor's wife at the Southern Baptist church, I realized I occupied a secluded and vulnerable position. The reality epitomized a silent and emotionally consuming post. My new station in life, which I had inherited because of the man I married, symbolized a domain surrounded by great expanses of water—an island. No incoming or outgoing vessels were offered. This island was not connected to the mainland by bridges or great stretches of roadways. I felt uprooted from the land of the living and planted in a desolate uninhabited place to dwell in a glass house. You see, I was on constant display for others to view and to judge my every choice and decision. Without guilt or compassion, others freely shared their judgments and thoughts concerning me with their friends and foes alike. I assumed the role of an island dweller, and by default was delegated the bulk of the responsibility of our children. I believe I equated the lack of time spent with my husband and the role as primary caregiver of the children as avenues of serving God. Adaptation to the required sacrifice was the position I was delegated and embraced. I would be a martyr for the cause of Christ by my total devotion to Richard Vaden. Without being consciously aware of it, I began an attempt to serve Christ through my husband.

In the purest part of my heart, I was serving the Lord; however, my service was through an obscure view that would be revealed to me many years later. This sacrificial role I assumed, which I had viewed as scriptural, was one of deception of the flesh and vulnerability. It was born out of an obedient heart, with the desire to please God, and interwoven with my unhealthy perception of devotion to my husband. Many manipulations and deceptions would be unmasked and uprooted decades later to reveal my addiction to and idol worship of a man.

Our new home in Aberdeen, where I lived out my sacrifice of service, was a two-hour drive from Corinth, our former home. I had maintained my friendship with my prayer partner, and we exchanged visits as we continued our bond in the Lord. We were invited to her home for one of those visits. A day or two prior to the visit Richard had one of his outbursts of horrific anger toward me. He said I had acted childish, so he was going to treat me like a child. (Note his perception of the way a child should be treated.) He got his belt and proceeded to beat me. When he had finished his lashing, I had welts, red marks, and beginning bruises starting at my hips all the way down my legs. Within a short time, I looked hideous with all the swelling and bruising. I realized I must conceal the horrible marks and bruises during the upcoming visit. No one could see what the man of God had done to me. Since I did not wear pants at that time, I wore a floor length skirt to hide his abuse. Again, by my actions or lack of actions I gave him permission to continue his abuse toward me. I was living in a world of deception evidenced by my lack of the ability to face where my life was residing. My life was in the grips of blinded devotion to an abusive man. I so desperately wanted a loving, happy Christian home that I chose to ignore reality. I lived in a dream world of the hope of what would surely transpire if I would just hang on. We were both Christians, and he was a man of God. Did not peace and happiness partner with those positions?

I encourage you, my dear reader, to soberly evaluate your situation of abuse. Do not wear blinders on your eyes, do not protect the abuser, and do not dwell in the realm of hopes and dreams. I read a quote from a narcissistic wife abuser who was asked to relate, from his viewpoint, why women remain with their abusers. His reply was quite profound and illuminating as he answered that it was because their hope is the last element to go. Face the dangers of the reality in which you are confined and seek help. If you continue to give the abuser control, he will seize the opportunity to push you down to exalt himself. He will always put his desires and needs above you and others. You and others will pay the price for his narcissistic behavior. When he belittles and degrades you or others, he is endeavoring to uplift himself. His mindset is so self-consumed that he is void of understanding the way he is wounding and destroying others. If he did realize the destruction, he loves himself so supremely that he would consider his behavior to be justified. In my fantasy world, I protected Richard's image to family, friends, and church. What I presented to the observing eye was not the reality in which I lived.

As in many Southern Baptist churches, two definite factions of people coexisted at the church where Richard was the pastor. One group was those who were the original founders and their families and friends, and the other group was those who came to the church through the outreach established by the new pastor. The founding fathers often resisted any program that endeavored to recruit new members. A distinct possibility existed that additions might sway the numbers to the point the founders would no longer be in the position of control. Maintaining a successful balance between the two factions took charisma and grit. It was no surprise that these factions were mostly in some form of civil disagreement and discord until both were ready for a pastor replacement. When both factions decided the time had come for a new pastor, they would become a united front to remove the existing pastor.

During Richard's pastorate at Southside, two pastors in the local Southern Baptist Association acquainted him with the Doctrines of Grace. These doctrines are sometimes referred to as the Tulip Doctrine or Calvinism. The tenets of this theology are total depravity, unconditional election, limited atonement, irresistible grace, and perseverance of the saints. He was introduced to other preachers in the area who also embraced this theology. Some of the preachers Richard met gave him books by authors who propagated these doctrines. In addition to others giving him books, he purchased his own volumes that affirmed these doctrines. His interaction and discussions with these preachers and theologians opened a door to Bible conferences where he met and had conversations with others who embraced those teachings. He was captivated by this doctrine and was propelled down a path of concentrated study into this realm of theology. Engaging in many lengthy discussions with other preachers added fuel to the fire of his examination of the Doctrines of Grace. This avenue of doctrine engulfed his mind, and he spent hours bent over his books studying and absorbing the fundamentals of this theology. Slowly and subtly after embracing these doctrines, he mingled tenets of the newly discovered theology into his messages at the Southern Baptist church. Before long, it was quite evident Richard was not preaching *pure* Southern Baptist theology. The change in his doctrine, propagated through his messages at church, was brought to the attention of the local Southern Baptist Association. A great hum was heard throughout the small town in an expeditious manner.

Richard, who was a capable student of the Bible, had studied the Greek and was not intimidated by the association. He proved to them that their association's articles of faith were founded on these identical doctrines. Subsequently, the association revised their articles of faith. The church where he was the under shepherd crafted a plan to call for a vote whether to retain or dismiss Richard as pastor. The congregation was in a stir and uproar as the forces against Richard collided with the forces that supported Richard. The two afore mentioned factions became unified when both decided to dismiss Richard as pastor because of his doctrine. The vote to remove Richard from the pastorate was affirmative. After the negative vote at Southside, an emotional time unfolded for us. It was Richard's first church to pastor, and the majority had kicked us to the curb. This separation was overwhelming for me. There was a small number of followers and some secret disciples who rendered their support as we transitioned to a different location within the small, nosey town. One dear, older saint called and encouraged me with comforting consolation, which I treasured. Prior to the vote, the old dogs of the membership let us know, in no uncertain terms, that we would be leaving, not them.

A staunch and longtime member appeared at the parsonage door one morning asserting to me in an angry and self-serving tone that he was there before we got there and that he would be there after we left. Another church member sat on my sofa and preached unto me in a very demeaning and unchristian manner. She proceeded to enlighten me concerning the errors she deemed associated with Richard's new theology. She expounded what she felt about Richard's doctrine and stated that she knew exactly what the doctrine meant because her daddy had believed the same thing. Her hateful attitude and lack of compassion brought additional pain to my already wounded heart. People acted haughtily and attacked me almost as quickly as they attacked Richard.

The casting out of the pastor and his family was an incredibly stressful, traumatic occurrence. I packed our things and cleaned the parsonage until it did squeak and shine like polished glass. I convinced Richard to return the church's separation pay, as I considered it betrayal money. We found a house to rent in the same small town and set out to plant a church founded upon the Doctrines of Grace. My heart was wounded for I was disillusioned by *good* Christians. Some smiled, ever so sweetly, as they linked with their enemies to orchestrate the plan for pastor dismissal. A struggle for power ensued, and the enemy enlisted his cronies to assist in our ostracism. These fine people wanted to hug me and tell me that they loved me, asserting it was not personal.

We united with a church of like beliefs and passions in a town twenty miles away. With this church acting as the mother church, we became an arm of outreach. Immediately, the search for a suitable meeting place for our group of believers commenced. Through extended family members of our congregation, we secured a transitional meeting place. We were encouraged and thankful to be a part of the movement to begin a new church. It was unanimous that we would be identified as Grace Baptist Church.

The appropriated building was a vacant country store in a rural community five to six miles from our rented house in Aberdeen and the former church where Richard had been the pastor. The old store building required some repairs to get its previously abandoned structure transformed into a suitable meeting place. The men of the church were faithful to come together to do the necessary labor. The mother church also helped in the aspect of readying the place appropriate for meeting. In short order, we began to meet as Grace Baptist Church in the old store building. The little room chosen as the auditorium in the old store building was packed with people at most services. The space tended to be hot in the summer and too warm in the winter. Although there was heat and air, it was not sufficiently regulated for the number of people congregated in the small area. Aside from the physical disadvantages of our designated meeting place, the congregation was happy and content. The advent of a new beginning and a new-found liberty, away from a controlling convention or association, was quite exuberating and electrifying.

Seven to eight families, some thirty to forty people, began to congregate together at this location as the body of Christ. Richard began propounding the Doctrines of Grace freely and without restraint. The parents of Amy's little friend from the Southside Baptist Church were part of the newly organized church. John and her friend's brother were also big buddies, so both of our children retained prior friendships. As young children, this blessing of their former playmates made their transition easier. I was thankful that my children were surrounded by supportive families and little friends.

On the heels of excitement of new beginnings, land to build a proper, dignified church building was sought in the rural community where the store building was located. A bachelor, who owned a sprawling farm nearby, sold the church enough land to erect a church building. Securing a loan from a local bank proved, at first, to be somewhat of a daunting task. We were situated in a small town, and Richard's dismissal from the large city church was public knowledge. In the final analysis, Richard was able to sway the bank president's original decision, and a loan to build a church building was secured.

The same landowner also sold Richard and me a couple acres of land, adjoining the church property, on which we built a house. We used Richard's military service to apply for a veteran's loan, which did not require us to make a down payment. If we had been required to have a down payment, we could not have embarked down the road of house construction. We decided on house plans and proceeded on the journey of building a house. Richard hired a retired carpenter to assist him in the construction. He subcontracted the foundation, plumbing, masonry, electrical, and other like tasks for the house. Richard and the carpenter, who had many years of experience as a finish carpenter, did the carpentry work which took four to five months to complete. My heart was happy at the prospect of a new house. My love for decorating had ample opportunity to flourish for the next few months as I chose a color palette, made all the flooring selections as well as the other design decisions. I stayed busy in the creative department as I fashioned curtains; crafted a hand-embroidered, hand-quilted bed ensemble for my little girl's bed; and one for my son's bed. I made placemats and other hand-crafted items for my new home. As I chose the interior design for each aspect of our house, I was challenged and fulfilled.

On the weekends, the men of Grace Baptist worked in a collective, concentrated endeavor to erect the church building. I cannot remember how long they worked to finish the construction, but it was a labor of sacrifice for them all. From time to time, the pastor and members of the mother church donated labor and services in a combined effort to help complete the church building. On Saturdays, to demonstrate my appreciation of their sacrifices, I would make a food treat to take to the church men as they labored.

Richard instructed the congregation on the Doctrines of Grace. The membership increased, although it was never large. At the pinnacle, probably the highest number in attendance was sixty people. Some old-time Primitive Baptists were supportive with attendance during those initial days. Our church fellowshipped with churches in the area that believed and supported the same doctrines that we did. Everything seemed to be smooth sailing during the early history of Grace Baptist. The beginning salary for Richard, as the pastor of a small congregation, was somewhat restricted. He asserted that I had to seek employment to afford our new house. I did not want to work publicly and did not desire to have a career. I wanted to be a homemaker and take care of my children and husband; however, at his urging and shaming, I went to work. I secured a job in a nearby town as a library assistant in a public school. Our children were in a different school district, so they attended another county school and rode the bus to school.

While I was employed at the public school, Richard and another preacher attempted to establish a private school connected to our newly organized church. Since I was employed in the public-school system, I received harassment from the county superintendent for being connected to a project which he deemed detrimental to public education. He came to the elementary school where I worked and spoke to me about the private school. I replied to his negative comments, and I told him I was astonished that the school board was against any attempt of educating children. The school board had no reason for long-term uneasiness because the private school effort was a total flop. Toward the end of the second year of my library assistant job, I became pregnant with our third child. John was thirteen and Amy was ten. The pregnancy was a shocking surprise. At first, I thought I must be gravely ill with a terminal disease due to extreme nausea, vomiting, overwhelming exhaustion, and weight loss. After consulting with the doctor, he confirmed I was pregnant. I was filled with great joy once the shock subsided. The school year was close to the end of the second semester, so I finished my duties for that current year. After the school year ended, I turned in my resignation and made plans to be a full-time mother and homemaker.

During the time the children attended the public school, Amy was required to dance and perform in some type of school sponsored music program. Richard did not agree with Amy being compelled to participate in the program. He reached the conclusion that the school had the liberty to force ideas and methods on our children without his approval. Thus, the decision to remove them from the public-school arena and educate them ourselves was inevitable. The memory of the day Richard went and removed the children from public school was forever etched in my mind. I was extremely emotional but supportive of his decision. My feelings of inadequacy to provide my children with the proper education were overwhelming in the beginning. Richard and I began educating our children John and Amy with the assistance of the man from whom we had purchased the church and personal property. He was a veteran schoolteacher, and he filled a position in our school for two or three years. He was an efficient, capable retired English teacher and contributed to the success of our school program. Eventually, other parents in the church decided to take part in the school program by enrolling their children. The aspect of self-educating our children was the initial change in the way we viewed world philosophy, its power, and its control in our lives.

John was born in 1967 and my Amy in 1970; therefore, it seemed as if we had started a second family with the arrival of Matthew in 1980. I had prayed that the Lord would grant me a child with whom I could stay home and nurture from birth until the child was mature enough to venture out on his own. Well, that prayed for child arrived, arrived, arrived, arrived, arrived, arrived, and arrived. Yes, your math is correct. It is not stuck keys on my keyboard, and seven little *punkins* to love and nurture were entrusted to me by my Father who is giver of all good gifts. Certainly, my nine children have been my good gifts and my crowning jewels of this temporal life. Oh, such joy and hope those little lives embodied as they sprang forth amid the travail and anguish of their births. God delivered them and caused them to breathe; thereby, demonstrating His power. I had wept and been resentful when I left John and Amy in the care of others to go into the public workplace. Richard had a history of applying pressure for me get a job by saying we would not be able to make it financially if I did not work. The Lord had granted my request of another baby, and I was exuberant. After telling Richard that I was pregnant, he began asserting that we would probably lose the house if I did not return to work. He tried to manipulate me to keep my job by shaming me and making me feel guilty. I believed he disregarded the provision of the Lord and implied that I had to be the supplier. I did not return to work, and we did not lose the house. God sustained our needs.

Matthew Spencer greeted our family in January of 1980 and was a joyful blessing to us and the church family. He was the only baby at church during those beginning years, and everyone loved and doted on him. John and Amy treated him like their very own live toy, and he afforded his older brother and sister great fun and adventures. Amy became his constant companion and buddy. I had not required Amy to help much with chores at home until Mr. Matthew appeared. She began doing double time just to keep up with her busy bee baby brother. Matthew was such a clown and was continuously involved with mischief. A determined little tot was he; he was not discouraged in the least when I disciplined him for being so inquiring and engaging. In momma terminology, he was into everything within his reach. Sometimes, he craftily managed to grasp things which seemed out of his reach.

Trying to conserve on our electric bill, we had foregone using the central air. Matthew would climb on the sofa where he could reach the air conditioning thermostat. He would give the little lever a flip to turn on the air. When the air clicked on, he exclaimed, "cool, cool." What a trip he was around two years old. He pulled another amusing caper around that same age. He could not tell time, but he knew what the clock looked like when his nap time rolled around. One day I told him it was nap time and he said, "No, Mommy, look at the clock." Mr. big britches had managed to reach the clock that hung on the wall and had moved the hands to a different position. He was determined and possessed an undaunted spirit. My little guy was smart and funny.

Soon after Matthew was born, Richard and I came to the conviction that we should not practice birth control. I had become pregnant with baby number four when Matthew was about a year old. We told Richard's mother that I was expecting and that we no longer practiced birth control. He conveyed to his mother that God blessed Adam and Eve and said, " … Be fruitful, and multiply, and replenish the earth, … ". (Genesis 1:28 KJV) Learning that I was pregnant so soon after Matthew, Richard's mother made a hilarious remark regarding the replenish the earth quote. MeMa responded, "By yourself?" In ten years, I would become pregnant seven times and deliver seven babies. Matthew's reign as the new kid on the block did not last long.

Before Matthew turned two years old, I was at the hospital in labor with Caleb. My labor was long and difficult. When I was taken into the delivery room, the contractions were close together with one contraction melting into the next one. Although I was experiencing difficult labor, Caleb's head had not engaged, and the membrane was still intact. The doctor became impatient because he thought he had been called prematurely to the delivery room. He decided to rupture the membrane and snapped in a harsh tone, "You just think you have been hurting." The contractions immediately intensified, and he ordered the assistant to tilt the delivery table to elevate my head. Caleb emerged shortly after the table position was changed. He was such a big baby boy with broad shoulders. The doctor quipped something like with those shoulders he looks ready to play football. I was so thankful my baby boy had arrived safely. I could have done without all the drama, but my heart was full of joy and praise.

Matthew and Caleb became best buddies as they got old enough to play together. When you saw one of those precious little guys, the other one was always close. Mr. Matthew sent his ambassador, Caleb, to perform dictates that he already knew were forbidden. My mother referred to Matthew as the straw boss after she observed Caleb and him playing. At that young age, Matthew was the one who took charge and called the shots. They were so connected as young boys, and fun and mischief were their middle names. The natural creek behind our house filled with water and overflowed during the early spring rains, and mushy mud covered the bottom of this natural waterway. It was a favorite place of theirs to play. Not only did they get wet, but they resembled chocolate-dipped vanilla ice cream cones after playing in the creek. I would usher them to the laundry room, which had an outside entrance, to take off their mud-covered clothes. Then, their clothes had to be laid on the sidewalk for me to hose off all the caked-on mud. This was an essential step before I could laundry them. Another adventure unfolded following the visit of a plumber who had come to repair a plumbing problem. They scrutinized the plumber as he did some work in one of the bathrooms. After the plumber finished, I noticed they were quiet and nowhere in sight. I went on a search expedition and found them caulking in the bathroom with blue toothpaste. The memory of their adventure has become hilarious— not so much then. With the absence of television and computer games to distract, imagination was running full throttle. The race to think of something fun was always in pursuit.

As toddlers and young children, Matthew had the outgoing personality and was the clown of the two. Caleb demonstrated a more reserved, shy demeanor. The children did not leave the house or church grounds often and were not accustomed to being around strangers. If I ever took Caleb shopping with me when he was a little guy, he would hold his head down to avoid looking at people. Gradually, they exemplified a reversal in their behaviors and temperaments as they got older. I saw Matthew transition from an outgoing personality into a more composed and guarded individual; whereas, Caleb's introverted shyness was replaced with a more engaging, communicative, and sociable personality type.

Caleb was an obedient child always eager to help with chores and tasks. At a young age, he displayed an extremely diligent determination to complete a task before stopping. He experienced bad headaches when he mowed the grass in the grape vines on our place, but he would not stop the task until it was completed. Working hard appeared to be a critical part of his DNA. This strand of DNA manifested itself in all my children, and Caleb's natural gait was at the speed of lightning.

As our family expanded, Amy became more burdened with additional duties to assist me in the multiple tasks of running the house. Later, she played a major role in the home-schooling effort. Her young life evolved into the adult world of obligations and chores. Due to the magnitude of all that was required to keep our lives in tip-top shape, she was called on to shoulder responsibilities past her young years. Amy was a consistent, conscientious worker and never complained about the workload she was called to perform.

An unfathomable amount of work was our way of life. She intuitively knew what to do, so I seldom had to direct her in our combined effort. Richard tended extraordinarily large gardens, and I would preserve the harvest. During the gardening season, my kitchen resembled a canning factory. I canned literally hundreds of quarts of food of different varieties. I canned one hundred quarts of green beans, one hundred quarts of potatoes, one hundred quarts of shelled beans and on, and on, and on went the one-hundred-quart list. I froze the foods that were better preserved by that method. I also canned fruit to use as baby food, and dried fruit to use in fried pies. One summer, I thought our apple tree would never stop producing. I made seventy-five quarts of applesauce in one day. It was a strain on my stove to be used continuously for several hours, and I ended the endeavor with a burned-out stove eye. I prepared assortments of homemade pickles and relishes for my family as well as jams and jellies. Harvest time started in the spring and continued into the fall when the sweet peppers for relish and the muscadines for jelly ended the canning season. It was impossible for me to finish all the garden tasks during the day as I also needed to complete the daily routine. After the children were put to bed, I headed back to the kitchen to finish the food preserving chores. It seemed the work was endless. The Vaden family was in harness to live a life of sacrifice and denial, often dictated by our religious tenets.

During the primary years of the founding of Grace Baptist Church, the Doctrines of Grace were our distinguishing theology. The embracing of those doctrines was the summit of our identity and set us apart from most of Christendom in our rural Southern area. However, doctrinal applications, some insignificant and some potentially life-changing gradually began to take root and emerge in the theology and practice of Grace Baptist. Some of the changes presented slowly while other changes were more abrupt and immediate.

The Narrow Road

In the early metamorphosis of the Grace Baptist Church in rural Aberdeen, each individual member approached the doctrinal changes in the privacy of his heart and mind. One personally and privately decided if a tenet should be received or rejected. The differences of doctrine held were not considered a test of fellowship within our body of believers during this phase, and there were varying degrees of adherence to the doctrines by the members. Some of the first practical applications initiated were: not using musical instruments during the church service, not having a television in the home, not attending public school, and not celebrating Christmas or any holidays.

After two to three years of the inception of Grace Baptist Church, those attending who did not embrace the evolving practices and doctrinal changes found themselves on the outskirts of the thrust of the church. Those precious souls slowly began to withdraw their support and attendance within the mainstream of Grace Baptist. Members who separated from the church during this period left on their own volition, not because the church body disciplined them. Our church became increasingly different and restrictive in doctrine and practice. Richard stated that those that left Grace Baptist Church were not part of us. He used scripture from the book of first John to support his position:

> *They went out from us, but they were not of us; for if they had been of us, they would no doubt have continued with us: but they went out, that they might be made manifest that they were not all of us (1 John 2:19 KJV).*

In my perception, Richard exemplified a narcissistic personality and became a domineering, controlling preacher after leaving the Southern Baptist Convention. He, however, possessed a persuasive, charismatic delivery from the pulpit which was a catalyst to draw the people of the church in the direction he desired them to proceed. When Richard began preaching, he expounded fundamental Baptist doctrine. His delivery was powerful. At first, he was a topical preacher, but he became an expository preacher, meaning verse by verse, book by book. No checks and balances from the congregation at Grace Baptist were put in place to limit the power and control of this man. As the pastor, he was the sum of the governing body of the church. I had, over the years, bowed increasingly to his control in the home and certainly had not questioned him regarding doctrine.

In the beginning years of our marriage, I spoke my mind and expressed my opinions or disagreements with Richard. These expressions and disagreements often angered Richard and, sometimes, prompted him to physically demonstrate his anger. If I did not have his meal ready when he walked in the door, he would get angry. He picked up a hamburger and threw it at the television the first time I failed to have his food ready when he arrived home. I realized within the first couple of months after I married him that I would have to make concessions if I wanted to maintain my marriage with this man. It was evident to me that Richard was not going to concede anything. Remember, my entire world was Richard Vaden which revealed my codependent personality flaw. I felt desperate to protect and continue my relationship and marriage with this man. I thought I would emotionally perish if he did not stay with me.

God has given individuals the ability to make choices for themselves. Dear reader, avoid relationships that demand *complete* allegiance to a person. Individuals should make decisions for themselves and not permit another to control them. I understand within the framework of a relationship, the two individuals should be compatible and seek to be agreeable, but in the final analysis an individual will answer for his choices. As a Christian, the indwelling power of the blessed Holy Spirit will direct and lead you as you listen to Him. God is the only one to whom we should give our entire allegiance. When you permit a person to be the filter instead of God, you are headed down a path of deception and idol worship. Ultimately, life choices should be between God and an individual. My codependence (personality disorder to render the welfare of others more important than your own) and mind set to render myself subject to this man's control were contributing factors of his influence over me.

The narrower the doctrine became, the more influence and control Richard exerted over me regarding my submission to him. He propounded scriptures which taught submission of the wife to the husband. I do not deny but embrace the doctrine of submission that is presented in the scriptures. Instead of defining these truths in the light of God's word, I believe Richard used these truths, as they were woven into the fabric of his message of submission, as a constraint and control of the woman. The guilt and shame of not following God's word concerning submission to the husband, *as Richard presented it,* was an additional means of control and restraint. Sometimes, after referring to scriptures which spoke about the woman being submissive to the man, he shamed the church women by proceeding to berate them as he condescendingly said that he had yet to meet a submissive woman, including his own wife. Richard had always exemplified an exceeding disdain for independent women, in any realm, who spoke with truth and authority. This disdain seemed to mushroom in the culture of his absolute control of Grace Baptist Church. The boundaries of a woman regarding her outward appearance, her attitudes, and her activities seemed to be a familiar focus in Richard's messages.

Eventually, church members had to be in complete agreement with all the doctrines set forth and practiced. Any deviation from any of the doctrines and practices broke the unity of the fellowship of the church. It is my conviction that the entire membership of Grace Baptist was slowly brainwashed to accept, unequivocally, everything Richard spoke as the truth. If I ever challenged or questioned his position, no matter how softly I had entreated, he called me the Holy Spirit to devalue and humiliate me. When he thundered from the pulpit not to touch God's anointed— referring to the preacher as the anointed—it was an attempt to silence and shut the mouths of any who would oppose him. No tolerance was allowed for a seed of doubt to take root in anyone's heart or mind concerning Richard's doctrinal positions. By Richard declaring that the Bible taught not to touch the preacher placed him in a category of untouchable. His doctrine forbade anyone to call him into question. He preached that God would keep him in line not anyone else.

From my viewpoint, Richard used the word of God as leverage to get his desired result. He laid the foundation for whatever precept he introduced upon a Bible text, but the interpretation and practical application he attached to the text revealed his opinion. By using the written truth along with some spoken truth that was interwoven with his interpretations and applications, Richard attempted to manipulate the members' perceptions. His desired conclusion was to ensure that everyone received all he preached as truth. Each tenet he formulated and each practical application he proclaimed became our doctrine and dogma. The congregation was totally pulpit led and ruled. To foster his control and domination, he utilized the Bible to instill fear. Richard alluded to such scriptures as the she bears devouring those that spoke badly about the prophet Elisha.

> *And he went up from thence unto Bethel; and as he was going up by the way, there came forth little children out of the city, and mocked him, and said unto him, Go up, thou bald head; go up, thou bald head. And he turned back, and looked on them, and cursed them in the name of the Lord. And there came forth two she bears out of the wood, and tare forty and two children of them (II Kings 2: 23-24 KJV).*

After the one hundred percent compliance to the doctrine was instituted, people either complied or left the church. Everyone had to participate in all the practical applications. The women of the church wore loose dresses with no waistlines or belts and did not wear pants. We were instructed that the meaning of dressing as godly women, meant to dress as Richard had preached with the long, loose dresses. When we first began to wear the loose dresses, we chose whatever print or color of fabric we preferred to make the clothes. Later, we were instructed to use subdued colors, and the fabrics had to be solid colors without patterns. We were taught that we were drawing too much attention to ourselves with the bright colors and patterns. The men wore solid color shirts and pants, which they purchased from retail stores, and they discontinued wearing jeans. I sewed constantly, as one certainly could not find clothes in stores to fit the requirements preached. Of course, a great deal of money was saved because I made the clothes for our large family. I made the girls' dresses, gowns, coats, and my clothes. I sewed pants, shirts, and coats for the boys. Amy became my assistant. I depended heavily upon her to help with the children while I sewed or cooked. My sewing room was like a factory in the garment industry. I believe the way we women dressed brought attention to us, because we dressed so differently from the norm of society. I remember an occasion while shopping with a friend, someone stopped us and made a comment. They commented that we appeared to be dressed in our nightgowns, because we were wearing floor-length, loose dresses. We had been viewed as spectacles instead of women adorned in modest apparel.

Our life of denial and presenting ourselves differently than society affected our daily routines. After the birth of Matthew, Amy was called to sacrifice much of her younger years to help me. She was not afforded much time to enjoy being young and carefree. I cannot recall her grade of school when it transpired, but she did two years of study that year. She began teaching school by the time she joined the ranks as a teenager. Her involvement teaching home school may have been when she realized her God-given gift to teach. Amy enjoyed her interaction with the school and the participation in the bustling activity with the little church children in attendance. While growing-up, John also realized work was a way of life in our home. He began working away from home at an early age. His first job was with a man in our church who was a surveyor. Later, he worked in custom cabinetry construction for another church member. Through years in custom cabinets, John gained many skills and demonstrated proficiency accompanied with knowledge. He was diligent in his work ethic and reliability.

Another area of our lives that began to manifest a difference from the normal practices of society was discontinuing the use of medical care. One of the faithful families brought a doctrine, which had been preached, into the threshold of practice with the birth of their third child. Richard preached that we should rely on God alone for matters of health. He translated the scripture from Psalm 20: 7 to support his theology that all help from men regarding health-related problems was wrong.

During the final days of this woman's pregnancy, Richard and I received a phone call to come to their house one evening. The husband made known to Richard that his wife was in labor. When we entered the house and passed through the kitchen on the way to their bedroom, I noticed a pan of water on the stove. My silent response was inwardly intense, and concern gripped my heart. In the water-filled pan were a pair of white shoestrings and a pair of scissors. The presence of those shoestrings and scissors in that pan of water demonstrated a mindset of this family to test the waters of home delivery. What had been only a verbal doctrine was about to be lived out in the real world of pain and blood. This scenario was about to become action, not just lofty ideals, and formal, stiff doctrine. These people were about to embark down a path of uncertainty; it was a path unproven by any of us connected to Grace Baptist. The mother had birthed two prior children who were delivered at hospitals. Her previous delivery had been a traumatic delivery with complications, defined as placenta Previa. This is a condition when the placenta separates prematurely and causes the mother to hemorrhage. The attending doctor had performed an emergency C-section to deliver the child and preserve life.

The stage of drama that unfolded in the bedroom that night involving the first home birth included a mother who had experienced a previous emergency C-section delivery. When it was established that the parents agreed that they desired to go forward with the home birth, the other church members were contacted to come to the house for prayer and support. The delivering mother, her husband, and the church women gathered, in the tension-filled bedroom, and began to call upon the name of the Lord. The men of the church uttered prayers and sang hymns in other areas of the house. It was a very real time of prayer and dependence upon God for His presence and deliverance. The birth of the child was uneventful, and no problems or complications transpired. The father of the child tied and cut the umbilical cord, and the little one was placed in her mother's arms. After a time of bonding between mother and baby, one of the women bathed, dressed, and returned the newborn to the mother.

That first home birth was a time of wonderful worship and praise unto the Father for His tender mercy toward us. It was a day of monumental beginnings of trusting in the name of the Lord not man. My heart had been fearful regarding the safety of the mother and baby due to her previous C-section. Amid all my fear, I turned my heart to God for His help. I can only speak about what was in my heart that night and the many times of complete dependence upon my God. My mind set and heart's desire was to please my God. The other people who were gathered evidenced agreement, and all the Church participated without any voice of dissent. My heart bowed to Almighty God's power and deliverance. I trusted in the Lord my God to help in the time of trouble and need that eventful day.

As additional trials occurred throughout this phase of trusting in God for our health matters instead of seeking medical help, I leaned upon His everlasting arms. During the time of the first home birth, Richard made the comment that he would be the person the authorities would seize if anything tragic transpired. He repeated this sentiment, usually to only me, as other life-threatening or concerning health situations presented. His comments embarrassed me when spoken in front of other church members because his words seemed to indicate that his foremost concern involved the protecting and saving of his own skin. After hearing Richard make those comments, I contemplated if he believed the doctrine he had delivered.

After the initial home birth, all babies born to families of Grace Baptist Church were home deliveries. We embraced seeking God for intervention in all health-related situations. A young child of one of the families suffered a poisonous snake bite on her foot and never received medical attention. The parents remained steadfast in standing still and waiting for the Lord's deliverance, although the little girl's skin turned dark on her foot and part of her leg. The children's social services agency was notified by concerned neighbors, but the child remained in the care of her parents. The agency made regular visits to the home until the child recovered, and she regained her health without any negative result. The home births and the snake bite were only two of the medical situations that faced Grace Baptist. Most of the men were employed in a wood-working business owned by one of the church members. There were two instances of hand injuries while the men operated saws at the business. One of these injuries involved a teenager and resulted in the loss of most of one of his thumbs. These injuries were cared for at home, and the injured men recovered. Instances of illnesses of multiple kinds with varying degrees of intensity occurred as we turned to the Lord for help.

My first home delivery transpired without incident and was the birth of my precious Rachel Grace, my fifth child. I had been up most of the night preparing a homemade relish for canning. Yes, I was in labor, but I was trying to finish my gardening task. Finally, I knew the baby's birth was imminent, and I aroused Richard. He had a severe headache, so I helped him get dressed and put on his shoes. My labor continued through the normal stages, and my awaited Rachel Grace made her debut. I referred to my baby as my awaited Rachel Grace because I had chosen her name when I was pregnant with my third baby, and I had anticipated her birth since that time. I believed her name had been put on my heart by the Lord, so I felt her little life would come to fruition. His presence was so real the day of her birth, and His sweet peace encompassed and calmed me.

By the time Rachel was a toddler, she was a very busy *prissy missy* with bouncy, blonde curls. I referred to her as my girl Matthew, because she mimicked his behavior at that age by getting into everything. The Grace Baptist Church women's clothes fashion had changed after the birth of my fourth child, and we wore only long, loose dresses. Beginning with Rachel, my little girls also dressed in long dresses. One might assume that being attired in a long dress would hamper the ability to maneuver and crawl. My Gracie Girl (my favorite pet name for her) was not intimidated in any way and managed crawling wherever she wanted to venture in her long dress.

When Rachel was about three, I realized her vision was impaired. The optometrist diagnosed her as legally blind, and she was fitted with prescription glasses. She wore glasses until she was old enough to use contact lenses. Rachel's heart was gifted with motherly attributes, making her a perfect older sister for her younger siblings. Nephews and nieces were also recipients of these gifts, which she instinctively bestowed upon them. She was studious with her schoolwork and did not require prodding to complete her assignments. Math was her bread and butter in school. She displayed excellence and competency in that area of study. When she did chores at home, she demonstrated characteristics of dependability and organization, as she had in her schoolwork. If her younger sisters did not fold the clothes to suit her, she would redo them.

Seventeen months later, the birth of my Lydia Ruth manifested with a traumatic delivery. Her birth was accompanied by complications that were potentially life-threatening for my baby and me. My labor was long and difficult. Exhaustion concerned me as I continued to struggle during the anguishing labor. Although I exerted tremendous strength and energy when I bore down and pushed with the contractions, no progress was evidenced. I decided some type of condition restrained the delivery. Finally, I felt something change inside of me. I was unaware, at the time, what had transpired. The Lord gave me the assurance that my baby would soon be born. She emerged bluish with the umbilical cord wrapped tightly around her little neck several times. The cord was compressed, because it was tightly wrapped around her neck, and had deprived her adequate oxygen. She was accompanied by the placenta closely in tow. Since most of the umbilical cord was wrapped around her little neck, enough cord did not remain to allow the separate birthing of baby and placenta. I think what I had felt inside of me was the placenta prematurely separating or tearing away from the uterine wall. Instead of the baby and the placenta arriving at separate times, they emerged at the same time. I began to hemorrhage profusely because I had experienced this complication. Those present that day and I began to call upon our God, our Deliverer. God, in my understanding, prematurely separated the placenta and preserved life by allowing Ruth to be born. The immediate and profuse hemorrhaging that had ensued with the birth of Ruth stopped abruptly. God my Deliverer had prevailed! When the cord was unwrapped from my baby's neck, her color changed to a normal skin tone. My great and marvelous God spared both my child and me. My heart was pure before the Lord that day in my dependence upon Him. He had protected my baby and me.

The eyes of the Lord search the whole earth in order to strengthen those whose hearts are fully committed to him... (II Chronicles 16: 9 NLT).

My Ruth was a very congenial and mild-mannered little girl. She had a ready smile and was constantly adorning her pretty face with that big, beautiful smile. Her siblings said she was always the one in the group who did not want to get into trouble. Ruth and Caleb were easily managed throughout their childhood. Although they were the two least likely children to get into trouble, they were the two hardest to get to sleep when they were little. Many years later, I think I finally figured out why they had been so difficult to get down at night. Since they had been calmer and not into everything during the day, they just were not as tired when bedtime arrived. My pet name for my congenial child Ruth was Ruth Goose. She possessed a compassionate spirit and seemed to flourish when called upon to help others. An excellent aptitude to consume knowledge was in her possession; henceforth, she developed into a capable student. Her ability for problem-solving and comprehension was extraordinary. These gifts enabled her to excel as a college student and in her chosen profession as a nurse.

Many instances of sickness and trials intruded into our pattern of life. I depended upon God's power and deliverance each time a challenging or frightening health-related experience revealed itself. By endeavoring to have a pure heart before my sweet Father, I inserted myself into God's equation. I attempted to demonstrate my desire to serve the Lord with all my heart by my willing submission to all doctrines and tenets of Grace Baptist, which I was convinced were scripturally required. It was the identical doctrine of self that was present in the Garden of Eden. Because of our sinful nature, we attempt to insert self into God's work. My heart remains full of praise that my Father knew my desire to follow Him. He protected my children and me by His tender loving kindnesses and mercy. The book of Psalms says He remembers that we are but dust.

Like as a father pitieth his children, so the Lord pitieth them that fear him. For he knoweth our frame; he remembereth that we are dust. (Psalm 103:13-14 KJV).

There were times the children had high fevers, times I had dehydration during pregnancies, a time I had excruciating pain with pneumonia five weeks before delivery, and times I had continuous pain and fever with chronic kidney infections. My chronic kidney infections and associated pain appeared to have been a result of advanced periodontal disease. My gum condition progressively worsened since it was not addressed; therefore, I believe I struggled with ongoing kidney infections and associated pain.

I entreated Richard to let me go to a dentist. He consented for me to seek help, and I had my teeth extracted without the aid of pain medication or anesthetic. The dentist was amazed at my resilience to endure the painful process which required two visits to accomplish. My endurance was possible only by the power and supply of my God because He alone enabled me to maintain during the acute pain of the extractions. The attending dentist commented after the process was completed that he certainly believed in prayer more than he had previously. My experience during both visits was a testament to God's sustaining power in the face of adversity. I completed each ordeal with calm and peace, never uttering a sound. God was my very present help in time of trouble. The people present in the waiting room during my first visit learned my intent that day to have my teeth extracted without any pain medication. They inquired of the medical personnel and asked how I had made it through the process. I pray they were told that I had depended upon God. My chronic kidney infections subsided after the extraction of my teeth.

Others of our flock experienced home births as well as illnesses and health crisis for which they turned unto the Lord. Choosing not to seek medical help was an enormous practical application for all who embraced trusting in God alone. The practice of this doctrine was the last straw for some members. Some may have been teetering on the fence of staying or leaving prior to the introduction of this tenet, but they left as this practice was proclaimed. They did not wait until a personal medical trial or test presented to make their exodus.

Many other doctrines also became part of our lives and practice. The women did not venture into public places without their husbands. They did not talk on the phone unless their husbands were present. These practices were a result of Richard's doctrine of headship. He had preached that women had to be in the presence of their husbands to engage in these activities, because we alone, did not possess the authority to act. Earlier, he had preached that women should not participate in a job or work position outside the home. The women were to stay at home tending to the matters of family and home. We eliminated televisions from our homes, along with radios, newspapers, and any printed materials except our Bibles. Basically, we were isolated from any outside influences or connections. We did not observe holidays, we discontinued the use of caffeine products, we followed certain guidelines in cleaning our houses, we worked from sunup to sundown six days a week, and we set aside the seventh day for rest. In addition to wearing loose dresses, the women did not use makeup, did not wear jewelry, and did not wear their hair short. Our families who were not a part of the church could visit, but they had to dress like we did during their visit. Visiting family members also had to follow all the other practices and rules we embraced while they were in our homes.

In conjunction with not seeking medical help, we did not patronize hospitals to visit sick family members or friends. My mother was diagnosed with a brain tumor during this period of our church. I visited at her home before she became bed-ridden and hospitalized. Mother lived in Kentucky, which was a five-hour drive from my home in Mississippi. I talked with her by phone daily as her condition worsened. Being absent from my mother's bedside and unable to minister comfort and care as the cancer ravaged her body, was a difficult, sorrowful time for me. My siblings rallied around her as death became imminent. The Lord was gracious unto me in the moments that she lingered before her home going. I was granted the blessing to talk with her minutes prior to the Lord ushering her into eternity. Our words to one another were sweet as well as emotional that day. My prior calls had been filled with encouragement and comfort; however, that final time I could not hold back my flood of tears. She expressed to my older sister that I had cried, which caused her mother's heart to want to bind up my hurts. What amazing grace she was supplied with the presence of the Holy Spirit during her sickness. Her life on this earth ceased only minutes after our phone call. I was told that her pastor remarked that he had never witnessed such a manifestation of the power and presence of God as he had during her illness and passing. I was reminded of the scripture from Psalms that states, "Precious in the sight of the Lord is the death of his saints." (Psalm 116:15 KJV) I did not attend her funeral since Grace Baptist Church members did not support funeral home practices.

New doctrines of forbiddance continued to sound from the pulpit. Richard preached that photos were graven images, so everyone was instructed to burn or destroy all their photos. We were to eradicate objects which were embellished with images or fashioned like a form of a person or animal. I did not realize that the destruction of these mementos would be so heart wrenching until the action transpired. It was a mournful time for me to witness all the photos burning in the bonfire. I left the fireside and went inside the house, so I would not see their destruction. It was agonizing to view those sweet mementoes curl and melt in the flames. My heart ached that I would no longer have in my possession sweet memorials of my childhood, my babies, or my family. Home decorating accessories, some homemade quilts, and articles of clothing designated as portraying images were also destroyed. Life continued to grow more basic and restrictive as the rising and setting of the sun continued.

If our doctrine had been closely examined, a contradictive thread woven into our theology could have been identified. Grace was considered the only avenue to God for salvation, yet we were instructed that we had to conform to the required tenets to please Him. The doctrine of obedience had been attached to grace stating that we had to follow all the tenets of the church to remain in full fellowship. We should have been examining the wonderful freedom that Jesus secured for us at Calvary. In Isaiah 61, God's word proclaims that Jesus came to give liberty to the captives. The requirement to keep the rules dictated by Richard Vaden placed an unfounded burden or yoke upon the believers. Grace Baptist Church members had been robbed of liberty and held captive by rules and restrictions. Instead of basking in our procured liberty, chains had been attached to that liberty. Our dear brother James in the New Testament instructs us that our faith will produce works. Yes, faith, not rules, produces works of the Spirit. No rules are needed for a child of God to bear fruit because it is an overflow from within. Our faith in Christ by the power of the Holy Spirit will constrain and move us unto good works.

Richard preached that a woman had to have a head (husband figure) to be a part of the fellowship of the church. He taught that a woman must go through her husband to please God. There were three women attending church who either did not have a husband or were separated from the husband. One woman was persuaded by the doctrine preached to leave her husband and not actively fight the courts for the custody of her children or house. She lost her children and home by default. My friend who was estranged from her husband moved to our area from Corinth to attend church. The church purchased both women mobile homes and placed the homes on the church property. These women served the church by teaching at the school, but they were basically confined to their homes the remainder of the time because of the *no husband* doctrine. My Corinth friend often helped the families that needed assistance during sickness of a mother or following the delivery of a baby. Richard's doctrine stipulated that a woman had to be with her husband when she went out in the public.

Two of the three women in this position were women who were initially my close friends. I witnessed their friendship shift from me to Richard the longer they attended church. He became their close confidant instead of me. One day, while one of these women was engaged in conversation with Richard and me, she commented that Richard acted differently toward her at our school than he did in my presence. I demanded to Richard that she had to go and that she could not stay in our midst. Shortly thereafter, her brother came and moved her to their mother's house in a distant county. She was the woman I mentioned earlier who had lost her children and house in divorce. My distrust should have been directed at Richard since it was his questionable behavior that had been exposed.

Not long after this incident, Richard instructed my Corinth friend to reconcile with her husband in order to remain in the church. My friend returned to live with her husband, but she was never the same emotionally or mentally. She started a downward spiral in her perception and wellbeing. Not long after she moved back home with her husband, she took her life. It was a devastating, tragic time for the church and her family who were part of the church. Members of her family, who were not connected to the church, placed the blame of her death upon Richard. They conveyed it was his fault, because of the doctrines he preached. One of her sisters wrote a letter to Richard relating that she, along with the remainder of her family, held him responsible for their sister's death.

Following the despairing events of the departure of these women, both mobile homes were sold and moved from the church property. There was a third woman who had a mobile home, but it was situated on Richard's and my property. This woman did not have a husband, and it was decided that she would live on our property functioning as our household servant. She and her son would come under the authority and headship of Richard; therefore, eliminating her *no husband* standing. What was I thinking? Yes, I needed help with the large house and many children. I realized, however, that bringing another woman under the headship of my husband was not the answer to my need. I could not function in that situation. The arrangement dissolved, the trailer was sold, and she and her son went to live elsewhere. I later apologized to the woman and confessed that I was sorry I had put her in that position. Grace Baptist Church had no other women in the membership who came under the category of the *no husband or head doctrine*.

While I was pregnant with my seventh child, I became gravely ill with pneumonia about five weeks before delivery. I noticed the baby's movements slowed down during the time I was so sick. I was extremely concerned that my baby was experiencing problems and might have difficulty at birth. Tiny baby Joshua was born late one afternoon and appeared undernourished. He weighed five pounds and looked like he had lost weight prior to his birth. I tried to nurse him and supplemented with bottles, trying desperately to give him sustenance. My heart cried unto the Father to cause my little baby to eat and gain weight. It seemed I was in the midnight hour when the Lord heard the cries of my heart. Joshua began to thrive and ceased to need prayers regarding his need of sufficient nutrition. He caught on to the food thingy, started growing like a weed, and had energy to spare.

Joshua was a very mischievous and adventurous little boy. When his imagination failed, his siblings readily offered their assistance. He was the child in our family that everyone blamed for everything. One time, one of the little girls accidently wet her pants, she exclaimed, "Joshua did it." When I did the roll call, his name would be first on my list. His actions and constant tricks challenged me and my sanity, but his heart was as big as Texas. Kindness to others was an attribute with which God had blessed Joshua. A willingness to help others always prevailed in his attitude. He fiercely defended me and loved me unashamedly. There were failures on my part to reach Joshua in school. He was such a smart child, but I did not know how to teach or engage him. God gifted Joshua with a wonderful personality that exemplified his compassion for others. As a child, he always knew all the neighbors near and far. He did chores for them, and they rewarded him with goodies of various kinds. I knew he would succeed in life because he did not mind hard work and possessed the ability to be enterprising in his endeavors.

My baby girl, Mary Elizabeth, was a sweet, undemanding child who stole my heart with her big as life smile. She shared her beautiful smile generously, and it was one of the assets of her beauty. One of my pet names for her was Sunshine, and another was Mary Lou. Her big sisters' opinions were paramount in her mind, and she wanted their approval on everything. Sometimes, those same sisters gave her a hard time. They knew that she was a neat freak (like her mother), and they, sometimes, purposely messed-up her neatly arranged clothes in her dresser drawers. She would cry and spend all afternoon arranging and rearranging everything. Teaching Miss Sunshine challenged Mrs. Lee, a longtime friend who helped with home school, and me. Mary implemented an extremely high standard for herself. Anything short of perfection was reason for a complete meltdown. Her childhood attributes of determination and high standards continued and catapulted her successful college education. Resolve and perseverance were two strengths that kept her fighting to reach her goals.

The last of the brood turned out to be the biggest of my nine babies, weighing in at 10 pounds. His birth was so abrupt that only one of the church women arrived before he was born. Jacob Benjamin, who answered to Benjamin until his teen years when he began referring to himself as Jake and later Jacob, was baby number nine. As a little boy, many times when I took him shopping with me, he would wander away. I would become frantic until I could locate my little guy. It became evident to me that Benjamin was blessed intellectually, but I was unable to inspire him to cultivate his full potential. He did not respond to my challenges and urges to reach for the stars. I failed to successfully reach him in the educational process, and I believed he was more capable than his achievement. His brothers and sisters accused me of spoiling him. They said I always let him have his favorite lunch food of peanut butter and syrup sandwiches, but I made them eat something healthier.

During the time we lived rules-regulated and restricted lives, Richard and I took getaways to the Smokey Mountains of East Tennessee. We took one or two trips a year, and our oldest daughter or other church members would watch our children. I looked forward to these trips as a time to let down from my many responsibilities. I did, however, prepare many lavish meals on the trips because we did not patronize restaurants. Our restricted religious tenets were practiced wherever we were. Many of the other church members took similar trips to the mountains, and sometimes we swapped with the babysitting duties.

A new restrictive doctrine often sounded from the pulpit. It seemed Richard abused the office as pastor to propagate his personal preference of others' physical appearance. He was repulsed by overweight people and often voiced his disgust. He had always hounded me privately and publicly about my weight. He set forth a formula whereby each member's correct weight per Richard's standard was established. If a member failed to meet Richard's weight regulation, the member was in violation and was not in full fellowship. Members not in full fellowship could not partake of the Lord's Supper. There was a stipulated amount of time a member had to rectify his violation of Richard's weight regulation to partake of the Lord's table.

At the same time of weight regulation within Grace Baptist, a child in one of the families became acutely ill. It was the same family whose child survived the snake bite. We received a call late one evening to come to their house to pray for their daughter. When I walked into the child's room, I was instantly shaken by her condition. She was delirious, and she entered into a coma from which she never recovered. The father of the child stated that he did not desire to go to a doctor even if he had to dig x number of graves. His statement seemed to imply he was not going to a doctor for this child or any of his children. The flock of Grace Baptist Church gathered at the home to pray for the gravely ill child, who appeared to be slipping away. The child never regained consciousness and died.

Richard went with me to the home that evening to see about the child. He, however, spent most of his time at the home lying down in a room across the hall from the child's room. While studying in his church office a few weeks earlier, he had experienced a passing-out spell. He complained of a loss of strength since that time. After his passing-out incident, he concluded that he had encountered a heart-related problem. Richard's symptoms continued for weeks, and he spent many days confined to bed unable to perform his normal duties. On several occasions, the church gathered in our bedroom to worship, and Richard delivered the message from the bed. Since he had preached the doctrine not to consult doctors for medical help, he feared that law enforcement would attribute blame to him for the child's death.

This young girl's death was a heartbreaking, anguishing event for our church and an almost inconsolable time for the parents. My heart mourned and grieved for the loss in this family. The proper authorities were notified to come to the home and make an assessment. Law enforcement required an autopsy, so the funeral and burial were delayed. When the child's body was returned to the family, she was placed in a coffin prepared by some of the men of the church. The funeral was held at the church, and she was buried in a local country cemetery not far from the family's home.

Return to Society

As mentioned earlier and not long before the child became ill, Richard experienced some type of health issue which he decided was a heart-related problem. Soon after he got sick, he began an about-face with his position on some of the doctrines he had preached, practices he had incorporated, and regulations and rules he had initiated. The return of musical instruments as part of the worship service was the first change Richard reinstated. When he returned the use of the piano to the worship service, he purchased an organ to use in conjunction with the piano. Several changes in doctrine and practice seemed to be weighing in the balances of his mind during this time.

Richard's sister and her husband, who was also preacher, learned of the child's death and that Richard was considering a regression of his position on some of his beliefs. They traveled from Nashville to our home in Mississippi to encourage and persuade him to make the doctrinal and practical changes he was contemplating. Carol and her husband, Jerry, attended our church service the night the grieving parents returned to church following their child's death. Richard stated at that service that he had reversed his position to seek medical help. He told the church he thought if he went to the doctor, then others would take the same liberty. It was the last time the grieving family gathered with Grace Baptist Church.

My heart was in an immense struggle during the visit of his sister and husband. I struggled because of the doctrinal and practical modifications that appeared to be on the horizon of change. My heart was overwhelmed with turmoil during this period of reverted change, and I did not want to dishonor God with an abrupt decision. I felt I had lived my trust of God during my illnesses, birth of my children, and other challenging times. I believed I had totally depended upon God for His deliverance. My heart and spirit wrestled with radical change that was indicative of the return to medical help. As I sought the Lord about this change, I was conflicted and pondered whether Richard had ever believed what he preached about God as the Healer of our diseases. It seemed he chose a convenient time to make changes regarding the use of medical care. This change unfolded at the precise moment he was faced with a health issue himself.

After Richard declared he would be going to a doctor, we decided to visit his sister. One reason we traveled to Nashville was to seek refuge from the negative publicity surrounding the young girl's death. People drove by our house and shouted, "murderer." The newspaper publicized adverse headlines with articles containing derogative comments about the church and Richard. A television news' reporter appeared at our front door and asked for a statement from Richard regarding the child's death. A dark cloud hovered over our church and over us personally. My heart continued to experience unrest during this time of reformation. Through a time of meditation, considerations, and petitions to my Father, I came to understand my implicit trust in the Lord for healing did not forbid me to utilize the skills and technology of men. God remained the preserver of life in all situations, and I realized there was no sin in consulting with a doctor. Had doctors been present in any of my frightening medical situations, their presence and performance of techniques and procedures would not have prevented me from completely depending on God for healing. I understood that I had the power and liberty to continue to embrace the truth spoken about in Psalms 103:3 that God is the Healer of our diseases.

Going to Carol's home in Nashville represented a freeing from some of the shackles and bondages by which I had been bound.

The years of withdrawal of our church from society had promoted within us a judgmental attitude of others' religious views. Since Grace Baptist practiced so many restrictive (legalistic) doctrines, an attitude of self-righteousness and holier-than-thou prevailed. The insertion of self into our scheme of religious theology promoted a superior frame of mind (pride). The doctrine of self or works in any theology consistently promotes pride. Our many doctrines with their strict, practical applications were for me an attempt to serve God in a purer way, but my pure heart did not need to prove anything to God. He already knew my heart and motives. In the scriptures, we have been instructed not to focus on the outward adorning, but to focus on the hidden man of the heart which produces godliness. Our heart should be the place change originates. If we submit to the Holy Spirit's leadership in our hearts, our lives produce an outward manifestation. The flesh is eager to insert self into God's work; therefore, we should guard against legalism and works of the flesh. We like being in charge and having control, and we are sometimes swayed by the flesh to perform works that we, not God, produce. We sometimes become silently boastful about the works that God does produce by withdrawing from others that have not attained to our level of *holiness*. Satan wants us to succumb to a judgmental attitude. All Christians are in a growth pattern, so do not be hard on others who are where you used to be and pray for those who do not know Christ. Tend to the matters of the heart, and compassion tempered with mercy will be the outcome.

My journey back to serving God with my eyes wide open was not an immediate, but rather, a gradual progression. Satan would like for Christians to believe that chains and shackles are easier to deal with than truth. Sometimes his deception has deluded our thoughts to perceive our chains and shackles are truth. Whatever direction he chooses to deceive us matters not to him because deceit is his game. On the other hand, truth strips us of our masks, and it strips us down to the raw places. It would take the unveiling of a dark family tragedy for the blinders to be jerked completely from my eyes. After the revelation of this tragedy, I faced the full deception by which I had been constrained for many years. The trip to Nashville included multiple facets: relief from negativity; a visit to a heart specialist for Richard, which revealed a healthy heart; purchase of societal acceptable clothes; and make-up and haircut for me. When we returned to Mississippi, we dressed and looked differently. Although still conservative in my wardrobe choices, I blended with the norm of society. I portrayed that one can be modestly dressed without being a spectacle. We headed back to Aberdeen, Mississippi, after visiting with Carol for a week or two. As time unfolded, additional changes were welcomed by Grace Baptist Church.

Within a few months of the death of the young girl, a distinct rumbling of dissenters' voices was heard throughout our county. Those discontent individuals approached the office of the District Attorney of Monroe County, Mississippi. They protested and made an appeal for justice. An outcry from citizens of the county, where we resided, demanded accountability in the death of the child who had attended Grace Baptist Church. Some of the former members of Grace Baptist Church were among those protesting. The people approached the Monroe County's District Attorney's office calling for action against Richard. On the other hand, they exhibited sympathy for the parents of the deceased child. We were told that some members from Richard's former pastorate at the Southern Baptist church, who opposed him years earlier, joined with the dissenters in the call for legal action against him.

One day without warning, the Monroe County Sheriff's deputies arrived at our house and ordered me to go with them in a patrol car to appear before the Monroe County Grand Jury regarding the child's death. I was taken to an empty room in the courthouse in Aberdeen, Mississippi. The Assistant District Attorney along with other assistants questioned me before taking me before the actual Grand Jury. After a barrage of intimidating questions and accusations, I mentally said, "Whoa, this is not the Grand Jury." I requested to see the Grand Jury who was supposed to question me. At that point, their bombardment ceased. I was escorted before the Grand Jury of Monroe County and questioned regarding many of the practices and doctrines embraced by Grace Baptist Church.

The parents of the child and Richard were charged in the death of the young child and were placed on the same indictment. The established charges were accessory before the fact of man slaughter by culpable negligence. As mentioned, when Richard announced that he would go to a doctor, the family who lost the child withdrew from our church. After their disassociation from the church, it was rumored that the parents made comments regarding the scenario of their child's death. We heard they perceived that the hours prior to their daughter's death functioned as a test by Richard for them. It was conveyed to us that they believed they were being tested by him during their child's critical and fatal illness to see if they would stand firmly on the previously declared doctrine of not seeking medical help.

Richard borrowed money from his mother to finance his legal representation and sought to retain a renowned Southern attorney to represent him in the man slaughter charge. The two of us journeyed to a small town in Georgia and conferred with the attorney. We entreated him to consider assuming Richard's defense in the high-profile case. After consulting in lengthy detail with the attorney, he related that he would visit our home and church before determining his decision. He traveled from Georgia to our home in

Mississippi to assess the situation. His visit in Mississippi was brief, but he agreed to represent Richard against the manslaughter charge.

Both sets of the defendants' attorneys met with the Monroe County District Attorney and his staff a few months later and agreed to a plea deal. Richard was not consulted before the plea bargain negotiations. At first, Richard told his attorney he was not interested in a plea deal. In the final analysis, both the parents and Richard agreed to plead guilty to the charges of accessory before the fact of man slaughter by culpable negligence. In exchange for their plea, the court non-adjudicated the charges and expunged all evidence of any criminal action. This meant that their guilty plea was not accepted in a legal sense by the judicial system, and their pleas were not entered in the record of the court. If anyone investigated the criminal history of either the parents of the child or Richard, no criminal action would be found on their records regarding the death of the child. Following the verbal entering of their pleas before the presiding judge, he declared in open court that if it were up to him, Richard Vaden would never preach again.

In a short time following the child's death, many of the faithful followers fled Grace Baptist Church. With the diminished number in the church membership, our livelihood could no longer be sustained by the church. Richard made plans to start a cabinet business to provide income. We sold the house in Aberdeen as well as the church building. Our relocation was thirty miles away to the small Southern town of West Point, Mississippi. Richard relied on the expertise and knowledge of our son John and son-in-law Aubrey, to assist him in the initial jump start of the cabinet business, and he promised them future ownership of the business. Both had worked in the cabinet industry for several years. They were talented and experienced in all aspects of custom cabinetry. Richard was a capable businessman, so he created a business which became successful in quality and production, by utilizing our son's and son-in-law's expertise. The business mushroomed immensely, in a few years, to a multimillion-dollar operation. He possessed a lofty vision, but greed, eventually, trumped judgment in his business practices. A lot of cash flowed into the business, but staggering amounts of expenses were incurred.

After moving to West Point, we continued with our practice of home schooling the children. Our school was located upstairs in the cabinet business building. Each student viewed the videos and prepared his homework during the time we were at school. I pushed the girls to finish their daily school program by lunch time. Keeping this strict schedule meant no time for extra school activities. One other person helped me oversee the school, and we kept a constant surveillance on the children. In addition to overseeing the school, I had the responsibility of managing our large house and family.

Managing a spacious house for a big family was a major undertaking. Upon arriving home from school, laundry for nine people had to be done along with tackling the remaining household-related tasks. I wanted the house to look perfect, and I had a husband that demanded a home-cooked meal each evening. I had to perfectly prepare all the food and have it piping hot when he walked through the door each evening, although I was never sure of his arrival time. The ax would fall if I failed in any area of his demands. Mealtime could be extremely stressful for the children and me. Most of the time, life at our house resembled walking on eggshells around Richard.

An additional rigidity of the home school involved our sons. The older boys would leave the house with their daddy each morning at six. They began their school process with their videos before I arrived on the scene between seven and eight. The boys' focus was not centered on their educational development. Instead, their focus was centered on assisting in the cabinet operation. Richard pressed the boys to finish their school tasks by mid-morning to head downstairs to their delegated responsibilities at the cabinet shop. Their school atmosphere was, therefore, in the hurry-up and get this school thing done mode so they could assume their tasks on the production floor of the cabinet business.

Benjamin, like his older brothers, was expected to work at the cabinet shop at a young age. He started with the job of pushing a broom. He advanced to sanding and continued to advance to various jobs at the cabinet shop. He was not supposed to operate the saws, but being the owner's son, he sometimes performed tasks that were not safe for someone his age. When he was about 13, he cut off part of one of his fingers while operating a saw. His accident upset me tremendously because of his suffering. I also grieved that he would be forced to live with the impairment the remainder of his life. Benjamin handled his situation remarkably well and did not complain then or later. He adapted and did not let the outcome of his accident limit him.

My job as the children's overseer at school was sometimes difficult for the children as well as for me. I believe my children would have benefitted from teachers other than me; however, at third grade level they used a comprehensive video program that had professional teachers. Their home school program was not geared to be a fun school experience. The Lord did not bless me with the gifts of a teacher; hence, my children suffered in the educational process. I pushed the girls to finish with school by lunch time instead of making school a pleasant, more relaxed, fun-filled experience. It was a nose-to-the-grind kind of situation. Despite the negative aspects associated with our home school, a good fundamental educational program was provided. The major failure of our home school was related to the atmosphere of their learning experience instead of the academics. The absence of outside friendships and activities to ensure a happy school day robbed them, to some degree, in their social development. The children's lives were not only controlled but isolated. They only interacted with other family members, church members, or people from the cabinet shop. The primary focus of our lives was consumed with work and absent of liberty.

During the prosperous years of the cabinet shop, we owned upscale, large homes. The first home we purchased when we left Aberdeen was in an elite subdivision in West Point. It was perched on a hilly, wooded lot. The traditional style home had a bit of country flare and was charming and inviting. It featured five bedrooms and four bathrooms. We gave the house a face lift by painting the interior and exterior. The kitchen renovation was extensive. New cabinets, appliances, and flooring were installed. Wood flooring replaced the carpet in the dining room and a lovely chandelier was hung. Not long after completing the transformation, we were offered a profitable price to sell, and we did.

After selling our first house in West Point, we built a large, picturesque traditional style home on a hill in a quality location. It featured six spacious bedrooms and five bathrooms. The master bath could have been the center spread in any home decorator magazine. It was phenomenal with a two-story ceiling height showcasing double-stacked windows, which surrounded the Jacuzzi. I added a touch of class by hanging an elaborate chandelier. The family room formed a separate wing of the house, adjoining the breakfast room and luxurious kitchen. This spacious area had twenty-foot ceilings, with a section of custom-designed windows that filled the entire back wall of this wing. One day, we found a note in our mailbox from an interested buyer. We negotiated and again made a sizable profit by selling the house. I packed our belongings, and we rented a small house in downtown West Point while we made plans to build our largest and most lavish house to date.

Richard and I took several trips during those lucrative years of the cabinet business to Switzerland, Greece, Washington state, Chicago, Canada, and California. We drove expensive cars; owned a river house in a gated community, which featured a swimming pool, a private boat ramp and dock; owned a ski boat and motor; dressed well; and furnished our home with high-end furnishings. From an outsiders' view, I am sure that it seemed as if we were living the American dream and then some. The last house we built was a French-country design and boasted some 5,100 square feet of heated living space. It was spectacular in design and amenities.

My duties as Richard's wife were basically to take care of the family and the home. I was never involved in any aspect of the oversight of the cabinet business. I lacked knowledge of the daily business operation and did not know the details of the financial status of the business. Richard often made comments during the final years of the cabinet business that the business was on the brink of failure. I did know that both our houses were mortgaged for the business, but that was the extent of my knowledge of the financial status of the cabinet business. From time-to-time, I was summoned to accompany Richard to the bank to sign documents regarding business loans.

One of Richard's shameful practices connected to the cabinet business was not paying our sons their wages for their work at the business while they were living at home. Our boys were required to work at the cabinet shop starting at a young age. He always said they got the benefit of their wages by getting to live in a nice home, drive nice vehicles, and other like amenities. Richard compared his philosophy of his treatment of the boys regarding their pay to a man who was a farmer. He said, if he were a farmer, the boys would be required to work on the farm but would not receive wages. Toward the end of life at the cabinet business, I believe Joshua and Jacob may have managed to keep what they earned. The children rebelled to their daddy's control and manipulation by leaving home as soon as they could. Many of the children ran away from our home to siblings' homes. John married young and left home. Amy also married young and established her own home.

When Matthew was about seventeen, he vanished in one of the company trucks. Weeks passed before we knew if he were okay, or where he was. Richard threatened to have him arrested because he had driven off in one of the company trucks. He personified an attitude of self-gratification when he spoke negatively to the other children about Matthew leaving home. From my point of view, Richard seemed to take pleasure berating one of the children in the presence of our other children. His actions and attitude hurt and embarrassed me, and I left the room when he spoke badly about Matthew. I felt this type of behavior from a parent to the other children did not please the Lord and created a tense atmosphere. Walking away from the situation was the way I demonstrated my disapproval. I should have voiced my disagreement to his face, but his doctrine proclaimed that I did not possess the Biblical authority to refute him.

Matthew had driven the company truck to San Diego, California, when he disappeared from home. He got a job at a McDonald's and lived in the truck. Eventually, a young Hispanic man he worked with at McDonald's offered him a room to rent at his family's home. After he had been missing for several weeks, Matthew called to let me know he was safe and working. When any of the children were in trouble or had a need, they confided in me instead of their daddy. I flew to California to see Matthew and tried to persuade him to come home. My efforts proved fruitless, and he did not return home until Richard traveled to California to retrieve the truck. Without a vehicle, life was difficult for him, and he was forced to return. Although he moved back to Mississippi, he no longer lived at home. Soon after his relocation to Mississippi, Matthew joined the Navy.

Caleb left home and got his own place for a brief time while in high school. Shortly after graduating high school, he married and joined the Air Force. Rachel sneaked away from home and lived with Caleb and his family while he was stationed at the Air Force base in Biloxi, Mississippi. Since Caleb allowed Rachel to live with him after she had run away from home, Richard shunned him. He considered Caleb's actions to be in direct disregard to his authority; therefore, Richard withdrew contact and affection from Caleb for a time. The remainder of the family was expected to react toward Caleb in the same manner.

Prior to Rachel leaving home, Richard made a down payment on a car for her high school graduation. She came by the house during the night, after leaving home, and took her car. Richard threatened to have her arrested for taking the car. He constantly tried to control and manipulate the children. His efforts to control the children stirred rebellion and provoked them to disassociate from their daddy. Joshua followed his elder siblings' actions by also running away from home. He lived with Matthew in Chicago for a short time before returning to Mississippi.

To my surprise, Richard allowed Ruth to go to college and live on campus. The college she attended was approximately twenty miles away, so Richard expected her to return home every weekend. He bought Ruth a car for high school graduation and supplied her with a cell phone. At that time, cell phones had not escalated to their present availability and popularity. Especially in our family, a personal cell phone for a child was not the norm. Not only did he demand her to make weekly home visits, but he also kept close tabs on her by phone. In addition to these tactics, he scrutinized the cell phone bill and quizzed Ruth on all the calls she had made.

I believe the children's rebellion to Richard's extreme control and manipulation is one example that demonstrated the expanse of the dysfunction that was present in our home. There was a public façade, which portrayed a family working together and worshiping together in harmony. This was not the picture of reality. Yes, we worked hard, but harmony was not the truth displayed in our lives behind closed doors. The boys resented having to work the long hours without receiving their rightful paychecks. Richard disciplined them with harsh and many times excessive physical punishment. I failed to stand up to Richard, although I did not agree with his excessive physical discipline of the children. I was taught through his preaching that I did not have the authority to override or intervene in his actions. One should not be manipulated by religious teaching to be forced to submit to authority. I was blinded and failed my children by not following my heart to stand against Richard when he disciplined wrongly. The presence of a still small voice nudging the heart that something is not right should be regarded as a violently waving red flag that the situation is not of God.

My mind was brainwashed to the point that I did not call him into question. It was clear to me that Richard ruled the house with unchallenged authority, which was void of compassion and justice. He was confident that I was not going to cross him in anything, because I had continued to keep him enthroned on a pedestal and had bowed to his authority for more than forty years. My allegiance and loyalty were reinforced by his use of the gospel to set the stage for his absolute control in all things concerning the home. I believe he took the pure word of God and used it as a constraint and manipulator of my thoughts and actions or lack of actions.

He knew that I loved the Lord because he had witnessed firsthand the way I had lived to please Him. My continued enthroning of Richard catapulted his behavior with astounding arrogance and confidence because he perceived I was under his control. I had obeyed the word of God as it was delivered unto me to submit to my husband without question. One day, the blinders would be jerked from my eyes by the revelation of unbelievable, horrific trauma. God would clothe me with courage and free my wounded, beguiled spirit. He would set me free from the chains of blinded allegiance. I would walk in Christ's liberty, the same liberty that He spoke of when He said He came to set the captives free and heal the brokenhearted. If I waited upon the Lord as Isaiah 40 states, my strength would be renewed. I would mount up with wings like eagles. I would be empowered to run and not be weary and walk and not faint.

> *The Spirit of the Lord God is upon me; because the Lord hath anointed me to preach good tidings unto the meek; he hath sent me to bind up the brokenhearted, to proclaim liberty to the captives, and the opening of the prison to them that are bound; (Isaiah 61:1 KJV).*

During the prosperous years of the cabinet business, we built a stunning three-story vacation house on the banks of a river. The property was situated within a gated community an hour away from our West Point home. Although we had a boat, swimming pool, and other similar amenities for entertainment, the kids did not enjoy the river house as they should have. The children and I realized that the retreat house was another place for more work. Instead of calmness and peacefulness prevailing the river house scene, the mood was tense and strained. Richard was often agitated by something I had done or not done that failed to meet his approval. I felt I had to be on guard around him. Home life, to a great degree, was apprehensive with uncertainty thickening the surrounding air. I am sure this tension contributed to the lack of enjoyment at the vacation house. A dark cloud would be revealed, later, that had also influenced the children's lack of enjoyment of the retreat house.

Through the years, Richard and I experienced many ups and downs during our marriage. In his fifties, I viewed Richard as a man obsessed with the inevitability of getting older. The aging process distressed and depressed him. He rebelled about getting older and displayed his rebellion in emotional, dramatic outbursts directed toward me. He, often, made cruel comments to me that were degrading and grievous. Sometimes, he expressed hurtful and atrocious statements from the pulpit. He told me I was old and looked old, adding that he did not want an old woman. Whenever we watched television, he made derogative comments about the women who were older. On the contrary, he lavished complementary words on the younger females. Richard sent me pernicious messages about my age and appearance as we watched television.

In 1995, I noticed that Richard pulled away from our relationship and engaged more with the children. At first, he focused on all the children; then, his devotion turned primarily to the girls. Departing on a family trip to the mountains of Tennessee and North Carolina, he told me to sit in the back seat of the Suburban because I had been replaced by the children. Not long after that trip, Richard asserted unto me that he did not believe he loved me. He said he thought our relationship was only lustful and physical. I was heartsick by his wounding words. I spent much time languishing over his painful concepts of our relationship. I concluded that he had replaced the attention he had given me for years, with the children.

When we took a trip to Disney World in Florida a short time later, his attentiveness was consumed on the children. This transfer of his attention and affections became more profound as time progressed. I had often heard when a marriage was troubled, one of the spouses, sometimes, altered his primary focus to the children. After Richard said I had been replaced by the children, I surmised this had transpired in our family.

I had tried for years to hang on to Richard and keep our marriage intact. I believed one of my duties to God was to protect my marriage and stay with the man of God. Also, my addiction to this man and our relationship was more important to me than my own wellbeing. It was almost inconceivable that I was blinded to the extent that I continued to cling to a man who was abusive and physically violent toward me. My dreams and aspirations of a happy Christian home were deluded; yet, I clung desperately to the fantasy. The idea of a happy, God-centered home had been my desire and great hope for which I had longed since childhood. Yes, fantasy, for I was not living in reality because our home and family life exemplified anything but a godly home. When you are living in the pit of deception, you are simply— deceived. I had ignored how he, by his actions, walked in direct contrast to the qualifications set forth in God's word for a man of God.

> *So an elder must be a man whose life is above reproach. He must be faithful to his wife. He must exercise self-control, live wisely, and have a good reputation. He must enjoy having guests in his home, and he must be able to teach. He must not be a heavy drinker or be violent. He must be gentle, not quarrelsome, and not love money. He must manage his own family well, having children*

who respect and obey him (1Timothy 3:2-4
NLT).

Richard threatened to come after me if I made him lose the kingdom of God. (He preached and maintained the doctrine that a saved individual could lose the kingdom of God.) Again, notice the emphasis was that his failure would be my fault. Throughout our marriage, I had been appointed by him as the one to shoulder all blame for the failures related to him or us. When the children were older, he accused me of trying to turn them against him. I pondered his accusation and concluded that our children could make their own determinations without my influence. The children were unequivocally competent concerning their daddy's actions; therefore, they could formulate their own opinions. My word, for years I had covered for, and not exposed this man, to the point of my own detriment when he abused me. This attitude of blame was another effort on his part to push me down and exalt himself.

Although I endeavored to hide the abuse, I was living in the delusion that I was protecting the children by attempting to conceal the turmoil. Deception is a weapon of Satan and will destroy your sense of judgment and perception. In the eighth chapter of the book of John, we learn that Satan is the great deceiver and the father of all lies. After years of repeatedly being told everything that was wrong in our marriage and home was my fault, I accepted and embraced that philosophy he had propagated. When my body evidenced physical abuse, I would make excuses about what had happened or say it was my fault. These examples are compelling evidence that I had been brainwashed. I had allowed another person to manipulate my thoughts and actions.

One time, Richard hit me in the face which resulted in a black eye. I wanted to leave the house and remain gone until the black eye went away. I did not want the children or anyone else to see me that way. It was not an effort to protect myself; rather, it was an effort on my part to protect Richard. I did not want our children to know what he had done to me. He was so bold with his narcissism that he would not let me leave. I tried to conceal the black eye from the children. When I was unable to conceal the black eye, I said it was my fault. Many times, he hit me on my head avoiding my face where the abuse would have resulted in noticeable bruising. Richard hit me so hard, on one occasion, that the next morning the imprint of his hand remained clearly visible on my neck and face. A church member asked me what it was, and I just commented that I woke up with it that morning. I should have told the truth; instead, I endeavored to protect my abuser, rather than expose him. Another time he was so enraged with me at mealtime that he shoved my face into a pie in the presence of the children. There were many episodes of his physical abuse, and the verbal and emotional abuse was an ongoing way of life. I pleaded with Richard many times to try to make our marriage work because we were Christians. I thought peace should be the fruit of Christians and should enable us to work through the problems. However, peace in our home seemed to be intermittent never constant. The children had become accustomed to me exonerating Richard, no matter what his actions had been. I now understand that my protection of him led my children to conclude that I would not believe them if they spoke badly of him.

When Ruth first went away to college, she returned home for the demanded weekend visits. She developed a close relationship with a couple of friends at college, and her interests as well as the scope of people in her life, naturally broadened. College life took its normal pattern, and Ruth had a life that included more than home and family. She started visiting home less often. Independence ensued with Ruth's life, as is customary when adult children live away from home. She applied herself with her studies and did well academically during her college career at the university.

In the spring of 2005 while Ruth was in college, our granddaughter Leah got married. The wedding destination was in the groom's home county a couple of hours south of our West Point home. Richard refused to go to the wedding but would not disclose to anyone the reason he would not be present for his granddaughter's wedding. He arrived at the last minute that day for her wedding ceremony. The entire scenario seemed questionably strange, and I clearly did not understand why he had acted that way. The wedding took place in March. In April, I understood his reluctance to attend Leah's wedding.

Silence Speaks

On April 14, 2005, my family's life was forever changed. My married daughter Rachel had arrived that morning at the house to help me with the household chores. Richard had employed her to assist me, and her husband dropped her at the house each morning on his way to the cabinet shop, where he worked. By the time she arrived, Richard had already left for the business that day. The morning routine had begun, but it was not long before Rachel came and told me something was wrong with Mary. She said she did not know why Mary was upset, because she would not tell her. Later that morning when Mary came downstairs, her face manifested a troubled aura. It was evident to me that something was wrong. I asked her what was bothering her, but she avoided answering me except to say she did not feel well. When I tried to get more of a detailed answer, she stayed silent and would not elaborate on what was troubling her.

As mentioned, Richard had gone to work earlier that morning. He had planned to attend the funeral, later that day, of the mother of a dear, longtime friend in our hometown, Paris, Tennessee. Fulfilling the obedient wife role, I called him and communicated that Mary was upset; however, I told him I did not know what was wrong, and he said not to press her about it. He added that he would talk to her when he returned home later that night. Richard, however, did not wait until he returned from the funeral to speak to her. He came back to the house before embarking to Tennessee. After briefly disappearing upstairs to question Mary, Richard came back downstairs and reiterated for me not to talk to her about what was wrong. He told me to just wait until he returned home from the funeral.

As the morning progressed, I saw Rachel upstairs crying. She said that nothing was ever going to be the same. Her suggestion to me was to keep busy working. She said Ruth would come home later that day. Rachel told me when Ruth came home, that Mary, Ruth and she would talk to me. I was almost overwhelmed with emotion while I waited for Ruth to come home from college. It seemed as if the clock hands were stuck to the clock face as my heart grew heavier and my anxiety intensified with the waiting. My motions were methodical and without purpose as I endeavored to busy myself as Rachel had suggested.

When Ruth arrived home that April 14, 2005, the four of us went into my bedroom, and I closed and locked the door. My heart broke as they, through sobs and tears, struggled to communicate unto me their stories of violation unto them by their daddy. They began by telling me that the night before, Mary had used Ruth's computer and had come across an email Ruth had written to her daddy. It was not graphic in its content, but one thing Ruth had divulged in the email was, "I remember the first time and the last time it happened." She told her daddy that she wanted to break ties with him, and she was leaving home. She told him to put her car in her name, and she made other similar requests relating to financial issues that would eliminate interaction between them.

Since Mary was a victim of molestation at the hand of her daddy, she immediately identified what Ruth was describing in the email. She called Ruth who was at work. Mary was so distraught with emotion that, at first, Ruth had a difficult time understanding what she was saying. As Ruth realized what Mary was disclosing, she told Mary she would head to the house as soon as she left work. When Ruth arrived, the two of them talked outside of the back of our house until the wee hours of the morning. I never knew that night that Ruth had come to the house. The two girls devised a plan for

Ruth to pick up Mary from the house the next day and take her away, while Richard and I were attending the funeral in Paris. I was supposed to have gone with Richard to the funeral, but he changed his mind and told me to stay home. When the girls realized I was not going to the funeral, their plan changed. Instead of helping Mary run away, they decided to tell me their stories of devastation.

Each of my three precious daughters was grief-stricken as she recounted to me the incidents of molestation by her daddy. Before April 13, each girl had thought she had been the only victim of her daddy's unthinkable acts; then, the email surfaced with betrayal and pain gushing forth with it. I questioned them as to why they had they not come to me when their molestation first happened. I listened tearfully as they related that they thought I would not believe them. It seemed as if my breath had been taken away, making it difficult for me to breathe. All the times I had covered for Richard in other wrong actions persuaded them that I would again choose to exonerate him and not believe them. My blind allegiance to Richard had contributed to my sweet girls not reaching out to me to seek a safe refuge in their mother. They portrayed absolute devastation and horrific pain as they related unto me how their daddy, one who was supposed to love and protect them, stole their innocence to consume in his own lust. We all wept that afternoon as truth unfolded with hideous, unimaginable revelations.

My heart was so wounded for my daughters that their daddy could do such inconceivable acts unto them. To become aware that the fulfillment of his lustful actions surpassed his children's purity and protection, the vows of marriage he had made to me before God, and the responsibilities as a man of God was past my understanding. In my mother's heart, I just could not wrap my mind around the fact that he sacrificed our sweet daughters' innocence, along with their mental and emotional wellbeing to satisfy his perversions. I believe his actions of the molestation of our daughters were acts of betrayal to the highest degree. Not only did he commit these perversions, but he lived in deception while he concealed his actions to me, his family, his business, and to the church where he preached.

When the heart wrenching conversation with the girls concluded, I was very distraught, but focused. I told the girls that I was going to confront Richard when he got back from the funeral. I did not whimper or become afraid, but I was emboldened. What a complete transformation for me to face Richard about anything. It was like a so-called out of the body experience. The experience was as if I were off to the side watching everything unfold. My courage was not mine; my new-found courage was a direct derivative of the power of God Almighty. I was not standing in my strength, but in the strength of the blessed Holy Spirit. The girls left the house because they did not want to be present when Richard arrived. Although they tried to persuade me to leave with them, I was determined to face him. They continued to urge me to not stay and wait for their daddy, but my decision remained constant to address the horror of the deeds he had committed to our precious daughters. Both my inner and outward man were strengthened by the power of God, and my heart and mind were resolved, by the presence of the Holy Spirit, to stand firm. I could not recall a single time in my forty-year marriage that I had exemplified the courage or strength to confront Richard, while boldly speaking the truth. I did not waver in the face of the enemy, nor did I turn aside from speaking the truth. God had His little child in the palms of His mighty hands. Richard, Satan, or any demon present were all held at bay that evening as I addressed the abhorrent truth of the licentious behavior he had heaped upon our daughters.

I was not at the house when Richard arrived home the evening of April 14, 2005, but when I returned home and walked into the master bedroom, I discovered Richard sitting in one of the wing-back chairs. His countenance was completely downcast, and his entire demeanor and body language shouted guilt, as if his body had the amplifications of microphones and loudspeakers. I did not see the narcissist, manipulator, and dictator of the family that he had always epitomized. He did not badger me because a steaming hot supper was not laid out on the table when he got home. His face personified the countenance of one who was guilty and defeated. By the expression on his face, he appeared to realize what I was about to reveal. My first words unto him were, "Richard, we need to have the most serious conversation that we have ever had." He did not act surprised or shocked by my words or commence to harass me in his usual demanding, arrogant manner. No, his reaction was one of expectance of what I said. He was the one who acted with compliance that night, not me.

Eventually, we engaged in a revealing confrontation of his confession as we sat in his Tahoe in front of the garage of our West Point home. I related the incidents of sexual abuse the girls spoke about to me earlier that afternoon. He replied that he knew when he left that morning for the funeral in Paris that it was all over, and that everything was going to come out. From the time Ruth sent her daddy the email, the same one that Mary found on April 13, 2005, he knew the revelation of the molestation was a walking time bomb. That was why Richard had acted so strangely at the time of Leah's wedding. The wedding took place shortly after Richard had received the email from Ruth. After Richard received the email, I am sure he expected the truth to be exposed. He was, most likely, extremely apprehensive not knowing who Ruth had or would tell, or when she would tell. He said when he was returning from the trip to Tennessee that day, he thought about having a wreck and killing himself. The following is a quote from a letter Richard penned on April 23, 2005:

"For a while I contemplated—death—killing myself."

Throughout the entire encounter, God sustained me to look directly at Richard and speak the truth in a controlled manner with power and direction. During our conversation, he stated, while in his search of the scriptures, he found no verses that condemned what he had done. I could not believe that he would attempt to use the Bible as his defense or use it to tell one of the girls what he was doing was not wrong. Insertion of a portion of a letter from Richard to a cabinet shop employee written April 23, 2005:

> *"It seems Butch, that people consider this type of behavior, as the unpardonable sin of which we both know that it is not."*

The following is a quote from a letter Richard penned to our son John:

> *"John, this kind of behavior is not ever mentioned in the word of God—And yet it seems this seems to be the unforgiven sin."*

After making this assertion that the Bible did not condemn his actions to the girls, he then flip-flopped to a completely opposite position. He maintained that God had judged him for his molestation of the girls. A few months earlier, he had lost most of the vision in one of his eyes due to a detached retina. He said his loss of vision was God's judgment to him for the molestation. I also told him I knew about the email Ruth sent him. He said he told her to destroy the email, but as God had purposed, she had not destroyed it. This email was the same one that Mary discovered on April 13, 2005. As our conversation ended, I told Richard that he could never be my husband again. He replied, "I know, I know."

Following my confrontation with Richard, I remained at the house. At first, I took my Bible and went into my walk-in closet. Richard appeared in the closet doorway saying he did not feel right with me lying in the floor. He said he would sleep in the floor of the closet, and I should go to bed. I said fine, left the closet, went into the bedroom, and sat in one of the wingback chairs. Later, he came into the bedroom saying he could not stay in the floor, and he had to go to bed. He said I could go to bed also, and he promised that he would not touch me. I could hardly comprehend that he entertained the thought that I would get in the bed with him. Righteous anger and indignation consumed me and flooded my entire being. I said fine and left the bedroom. The study of our house transformed into my refuge as I waited for the dawn of the next day, never closing my eyes in sleep.

The last conversation I had with Richard was in the bathroom of our house in West Point the following morning, April 15, 2005. He kept asking me what I wanted him to do. I replied I did not know what his condition with God was, but I believed he had sown to the flesh, and he would have to reap of the flesh. I told him I did not know what I was going to do. I said I cannot tell the boys ... he interrupted me declaring, "No, you cannot tell the boys, you cannot tell the business, and you cannot tell the church." He misinterpreted what I was saying about not telling the boys. At that point, I was afraid if the boys knew what their daddy had done to their sisters they might be compelled to do something foolish that would bring harm unto them. He also asked me to forgive him, but with the onset of overwhelming pain accompanying the knowledge of the molestation, I certainly was not ready to consider the weighty matter of forgiveness. He requested for me to get the girls together, so he could ask them for their forgiveness. I told him that they did not want to see him. I told him to get his business in order and leave, just leave. In my heart and by my words, I was telling him we were finished. I wanted him to do whatever he needed to do to set our finances and business things in order because our marriage was over. He left the house that morning, and I made the decision to notify others of his actions to our daughters.

After the conversation with Richard the morning of April 15, 2005, I called some of the church members to meet me at one of the member's houses. My oldest daughter, Amy, went with me to talk to the church people. On the way to that meeting, I saw Richard in his Tahoe, on the side of the road, talking with our oldest child John. I later learned that Richard had also confessed a portion of his guilt earlier that morning to John. He had called John to meet him on the roadside and bring him some cash from the business, because he was planning to leave town. When I met with the church members, I told them Richard had molested three of our daughters. Everyone was shocked but listened. They seemed to believe my very emotional delivery of events.

Following the revelation to the church members of the abuse of our daughters, we headed to my oldest daughter's house; it was less than a mile from my home. On the way to her house, we stopped at home to pick up my youngest child, Benjamin. At this point, he had not been told of the terrible things his daddy had done to his sisters. My oldest daughter, Amy, went upstairs to get Benjamin, but before they returned downstairs, Richard arrived. I was fearful and anxious not knowing what to expect if Richard and Benjamin saw one another. My mind and emotions were reeling by this time. I wanted to avoid any confrontation that might ensue if the molestation was discovered by Benjamin while Richard was in the house. Richard mentioned to me that he thought the police might be trying to locate him, so he left rather quickly. The Lord protected us because Richard left before Amy and Benjamin came downstairs. Amy, Benjamin, and I headed down the road to her house where we stayed for the next few days. The girls were very emphatic that they did not want to go back to our house. They did not feel safe there and did not like the idea of being where their daddy had been the controller of all things. Rachel and her family also stayed at Amy's during this time, and her house served as a refuge for family and close friends.

I, upon the supportive urging of my son Matthew, contacted my son Caleb by internet since he was deployed to his Air Force duty station in South Korea. My contact to Caleb was an extremely emotional conversation. Unsuspecting of any of the unveiling of events of the molestation that had unfolded for the past two days, Caleb reacted to the news as if he had been slammed to the floor by a nearly fatal blow. Initially, he was attacked by the forces of evil, as I related the horrific events of the molestation of the girls. He was overwhelmed by the news of what his daddy had done to his sisters. Although he had been delivered a crushing blow, Caleb was sustained by the mighty power of the Holy Spirit.

He later emailed:

Hey, Caleb here. I know that everything is very confusing and painful right now, but I ask that you all keep me informed. I wish that I could be there for each of you. Just know that He has a plan for all his children and will make a way of escape for them. I love you all so much. I know that you feel pain because I feel that very same pain. I was in unbelief when I first heard the news, then I went into a very un-Christ like rage filled with anger that I have never experienced in my life. Then, God felt the need to make me feel trapped, because I am stuck here on this peninsula. Last night, one of my Christian friends dragged me kicking and screaming to a praise and worship service. Even though that was the best place for me, I did not want any part of it. You know, that was the best service I have been to in a long time! We sang a song, it says "Lord, you know me, and you know that I am at the bottom, and I do not have the words to even say a prayer...all I can say is Holy...Holy...Holy is your name." That is all I could say. God fill me with your righteousness, so there will not be any room for hatred, malice, or anything of myself. I think that so many times we are filled with ourselves. We lose focus on what God has for us. This is but another test, how will we fare? I have faith that my God will take me...us through this. I know that it is so easy to be mad and place blame and believe me I know firsthand. Last night, in the midst of my anger, God spoke to me saying, "and you and your sins are not worthy of hell?" I...we all are in debt to the King of Kings. So, as hard as it may seem, start praising the Lord for all he has done and blessed you with. Thank him for the trial; he wants his children to grow closer to him. I know that I am not a minister by any means, but I thought you all could use a word of encouragement! Caleb admonished us: *"Please, keep the FAITH. Our suffering is but temporary, lives are but a blink of an eye...eternity will be great with our King!"*

He added a PS:

"Mom you are a special person. and you give me and everyone around you more strength than any one person ever could. You stand in the face of it all with such courage and Faith. You are truly an inspiration. You are, without a

doubt, the greatest Christian I have ever known. God has a special place waiting for you. I will be there for you as a son and as a brother in Christ. Mom, I have witnessed you pass a many of God's tests for you, this is yet but another, to strengthen your faith. May God be with you all."

Our family assembled at Amy's house on the evening of April 15, 2005. We gathered to console one another and to talk about the tragic events of the girls' molestation that had been unveiled the previous day. We wept, prayed, and discussed what actions to pursue. Our tears flowed as if from broken water faucets. Phone calls were made to consult and seek advice. Ruth stated that she was going to report Richard to law enforcement no matter what anyone else did. Despite our tearful discussions and advice of others, our hearts continued to feel weighted down with the magnitude of the burden. Prayer was the unequivocal avenue that enabled us to go forward. From the onset of the revelation, we all knew what needed to be done, and there was never a moment we were in conflict regarding reporting the molestation to law enforcement. We had to, through prayer, physically face the burden with peace and calm and by the power of the blessed Holy Spirit proceed.

All the children and I went to the Clay County Sheriff's Department in West Point, Mississippi, and made official statements the following day, Saturday, April 16, 2005. I was advised of the seriousness of our actions by the Clay County Sheriff. The Department of Clay County Human Services was contacted, and a representative was present for the giving of our statements. The giving of these statements to the authorities was concurrently overwhelming and relieving.

Rachel said, as she exited the room after giving her statement, it was as if a big burden had caught on the doorway of the room and crashed to the floor. We all experienced some evidence of relief as the truth was revealed. I know this may sound strange that one would experience relief amid such unimaginable devastation. Truth has a powerful effect on all who embrace it. The scenario was as if the scab had been removed from a horrifically infected wound, and the pus and debris started to ooze forth. The putrefaction that had been building in our lives through the occurrence of events throughout many years was purged. All the lies and dark secrets that had been swept under that *proverbial rug* were exposed. *Truth* had set us free. No longer did a need exist to guard secrets, words, or thoughts.

> *And you will know the truth, and the truth will set you free (John 8:32 NLT).*

I understood that the power of God, through His Word, would set one free spiritually, and then I experienced that truth in all aspects of life was freeing. We experienced the exposing and emptying of an inner prison where we had been held captive. The concealing of truth had been devastating and had been a perpetual prison to us, the victims. With the revelation of the truth of an overwhelming tragedy, the gates of the prison were flung open. The revelation of the molestation was the truth that forced those prison gates open, and once those gates had been flung open, multiple rivers of hidden truth gushed forth. As the chains and shackles of fear and oppression were loosed, raw and unfiltered truth rapidly unfolded in our lives. It was painfully crushing to face the truth. Many times when truth is revealed it is accompanied by paralyzing agony. None the less, liberty of the mind and soul has a healing result when truth is revealed. The process was abrupt and unforgiving in its revelation; it presented with bursts of gasping, breathless moments. Moments of inconsolable anguish transpired repeatedly for several days for all the family and close friends. Our anguish was evidenced by our tear-stained faces and aching hearts. In the physical, a purging and cleansing of a physically infected wound is necessary for healing to occur. The purging and cleansing of an emotional wound must also transpire before a time of healing for the wounded soul can begin.

Richard was located by law enforcement and asked to report to the local Clay County Sheriff's office in West Point. He was read his Miranda rights which he signed. Then, he gave his taped statement to Deputy Sheriff Billy Perkins. The compact disk (CD) recording and the typed transcript of the CD containing his statement to the Clay County Sheriff's Deputy were given to the area District Attorney's office. The CD and statement were also accessible to Richard's attorneys. After the trial, the original CD and typed transcript of the CD were secured along with the other exhibits of the State of Mississippi v. Vaden, Cause No. 2005-031(Noxubee Cty. Circuit Ct. 2006). Concluding his statement, Richard was booked on charges of fondling and held in the Clay County Jail. In the following quotations from the trial transcript of the above stated State of Mississippi v. Vaden, Cause No.2005-031 (Noxubee Cty. Circuit Ct. 2006), Q. represents the state prosecutor's questions and the A. represents the defendant Richard Vaden's answers.

"Q. When you gave this statement on April 16th of 2005, it was shortly after you had been confronted by your wife, was it not?
 A. She confronted me on Thursday. This was Saturday afternoon at 5:00.
Q. And it was when you were still thinking that maybe your family was not going to turn you in, and we're all going to handle this amongst the family, right?

A. I don't know how to answer that. No, I don't know what you're asking.

Q. You never dreamed that your wife of 40 years and your children were actually going to turn you into the law, did you?

A. I had a realization that day I was sitting there somebody had.

Q. Before you were sitting there giving that confession, you never dreamed that your wife of 40 years and your children were going to actually turn you in, did you?

A. No.

Q. And it wasn't until after you sat in the Clay County jail for over 48 hours that you finally realized, whoa I'm losing control." (Tr. at 495:7-28).

After Richard was charged with a felony and sat in jail in Clay County for forty-eight hours, his denial and backtracking of his guilt of the molestation of his daughters commenced. While in Clay County Jail, he petitioned law enforcement to make a second statement to the Clay County Sheriff's Deputy. In his second statement, he tried to explain away and recant his admissions in his first statement.

Subsequent to his felony charges in Clay County, Mississippi, and forty-eight hours in the Clay County Jail, Richard retained an attorney to represent him. He used the only credit card we had that held me equally responsible for charges to post bail and retain an attorney. He stated during the divorce depositions that he would not agree to have my name removed from this credit card as an equally responsible party for the debt. He stated that he chose that credit card because I was responsible for putting him in jail; therefore, I should be responsible for the debt. Richard demonstrated his normal transfer of blame to me. He attempted to sidestep his guilt and responsibility instead of accepting the consequences for his perverted deeds.

Having completed the formalities in Clay County, Mississippi, we were advised to go to Noxubee County, Mississippi, to make statements. The sexual abuse of the three girls had occurred in Noxubee County, at the river house property. The girls, my son John, and I made the hour journey to the Noxubee County Sheriff's office the next day to file the statements against Richard. Once again, the girls and I had to make statements relating the horrific events of their molestation. After Richard posted bail in Clay County, he was transported to Noxubee County to face criminal charges. With an attorney in tow, Richard did not confess or make any statements when he was charged with fondling of the girls in Noxubee County, Mississippi. When his bail was posted, he was released from the Noxubee County Jail. The entire process for bookings, transfer, and release only took a few days. An order of protection was filed prohibiting him from coming near or speaking to any of the children or me.

The letters he soon penned to me and others, mirrored references to his guilt. He continuously incriminated himself as he wrote the numerous letters endeavoring to establish his innocence. During the following months, the letters Richard penned unto me and others demonstrated he had not comprehended the gravity or finality of my words on the evening of April 14, 2005, when I told him he could never be my husband again.

Following the statements by the family to law enforcement, we were unsure how Richard would react to us after he was released on bail. He owned some guns, which he kept in his Tahoe, and the fact of him having the guns frightened the family as well as some of the church members. While we were staying at my daughter's following Richard's release from jail, he drove by the house very slowly one day. His appearance on the road in front of the house was terrifying to the family because we did not know what he might attempt to do to us. One of the church members expressed his concern to the District Attorney's office with reference to the guns Richard kept in his vehicle. After Richard got out of jail, he retreated to the upstairs of the cabinet business after it closed each day. I believe he did not seek a permanent residence because he thought he would soon return home. I had always overlooked his wrong doings, and I believe he thought I would once again overlook them. He kept a low profile during the operating hours of the business, staying completely out of sight. At some point, Richard rented an apartment.

Some months prior to the events of the molestation revelation, Benjamin experienced some difficulty. I did not understand why Richard decided not to seek help for our son. After the molestation of the girls was uncovered, I understood why Richard had avoided pursuing assistance. I believe Richard feared that seeking help would have potentially exposed his own evil deeds and placed himself in jeopardy. He chose to ignore our son's need, because he realized an investigation and probing into the Vaden home could have conceivably led to the uncovering of his dysfunction within the family as well as his sexual misconduct toward our daughters. He simply chose to protect himself because the evil deeds of darkness avoid the light.

Not only did we deal with the wounding trauma concerning the girls, but we also continually faced people from the small towns of West Point and Columbus, Mississippi. Richard's molestation of our daughters was headline news in the newspapers in Clay County as well as the surrounding Mississippi counties. Our travesty was also reported in the news of our home state of Tennessee. The local newscasts on television news programs vented our tragedy. News concerning the depravity of man seems to flood the media through all outlet sources, and the appetite of the public feasts upon the reports of the same.

Whether I went to the grocery, church, or any place during the early publications of our heartbreaking story, I felt as if I were wearing a flashing neon sign that identified who I was. The experience was painful and rendered me emotional wounds. In my state of mind, and with my old prevailing companion the cloak of unworthiness, I assumed that everyone I saw or had contact with viewed me as part of the disgrace. Although invisible to the eyes of others, a very real emotional veil of shame covered me because I was connected in such a distinct manner to a man, a preacher, a husband, and a father who had committed the unthinkable to his (our) daughters. As people began to reach out to me and support me, I realized that I had sold many short. God held me closely through others as they manifested the best of humanity to me. I sought to maintain a focused determination to see this ordeal, including its ramifications, to its culmination. The first item that appeared on my agenda following the reporting of the molestation to law enforcement was to retain an attorney and file for divorce.

During the divorce preparation and criminal trial, I was sarcastically reprimanded by one of Richard's attorneys for filing for divorce so quickly. During the criminal trial, one of the defense attorneys alleged my divorce was part of a preplanned attempt to seize the Triangle Cabinet Business. I pondered why would any parent hesitate to distance himself from the guilty party who had sexually abused three of their daughters. Why would a parent fail to dissolve a marriage when the other partner had stooped to such a depraved form of sexual immorality against his children? My spiritual and moral indignation was insulted by the attorney's brash and disparaging perception and comments. I did not take divorce lightly. The history of my marriage of forty-two years in the light of the physical, emotional, and spiritual abuse I had endured throughout those years spoke to my convictions regarding marriage. With the revelation of my daughters' sexual abuse, I knew I could no longer abide in my marriage. The Lord emphatically moved in my heart to publicly dissolve the marriage that had been destroyed by Richard's perverted sexual behavior. In my heart, my conviction was that I needed to make a public declaration by divorce of the private severing of our marriage bond by the Lord. The dissolving of the bond had already transpired due to Richard's licentious behavior. I proactively endeavored to render all my energies, with which God would endow me, to encourage and love my precious girls as we faced the ramifications of his prior hideous acts.

Richard and I had a joint personal checking account and a joint account labeled R & B (Richard and Betty). There was almost a $12,000-dollar combined balance of the accounts which I withdrew. I used a portion of those bank balances to retain a Christian attorney in West Point to file for divorce. I used the remainder of the money to finance counseling for the girls and me as well as provide living expenses. I had no idea how lengthy, detailed, or costly the divorce would become. My attorney was appalled at the horrific acts Richard had committed against the girls that prompted me to file for divorce. I also related to him my abuse, both physical and verbal, which I suffered over the course of our 40 plus years of marriage. I filed for divorce within a few days of becoming aware of the girls' molestation by their daddy. Several divorce hearings, filings, motions, and communications between our attorneys ensued for the remainder of 2005 continuing into 2006. Along with the court appearances, depositions were taken by both attorneys from witnesses to give an account of certain facts. Richard and I were present at the depositions which were held at my attorney's law firm. It was lengthy and emotionally draining to engage in and walk through the procedures of the divorce.

Before entering the conference room of my attorney for the first deposition, I was extremely anxious and fearful. I dreaded being in the same room with Richard Vaden. The encounter when I confronted Richard about his molestation of the girls was the first time, I had ever stood up to him in truth. That incident was the most radical and fearless effort on my part to bring him into an account of his actions—ever. Now once again, I faced him. My attorney's office personnel encouraged me and offered words of comfort. Knowing that truth would continue to set me free gave me strength to go forward with the deposition.

> *...If God is for us, who can ever be against us (Romans 8:31 NLT)?*

Fear found no seat at the conference table where Richard, the attorneys, the recording clerk, and I were seated. The power of God, through the presence of the Holy Spirit, was in demonstration of His might and strength. All my fear fell in a crumple like a heap of dirty laundry at the threshold of the door of that room. Fear remained off limits during the entire deposition session. I was emboldened by my great Warrior as the enemy hurled fiery darts at me. Let it be testified that the enemy was powerless over me that day. My eyes never once shied from looking directly at Richard or his attorney when I recounted all the horrific events of the molestation of our daughters. I stood firm and unyielding as I recalled the many years the children and I were manipulated and coerced by Richard. I gave detailed accounts of his abuse toward me including humiliating comments he had made both privately and publicly about my weight or age. Without wavering, I recalled many acts of his violent behavior toward me. Basically, I was questioned by the opposing attorney concerning my life with Richard Vaden during our 40 plus years of marriage. My opinion was that Richard's divorce attorney's approach to me was interwoven with sarcasm.

In a different session, Richard was questioned by my attorney regarding the molestation as well as other life events, finances, his behavior toward the children and me, and any other aspects that would have had any bearing on the divorce. Throughout Richard's deposition, he attempted to play down most of his violent acts toward me. Sometimes, he conveniently said he did not remember. He loudly proclaimed his unyielding promise that he would love me and financially support me all my life. Of course, he pled the fifth on questions concerning the molestation. The depositions took place in December of 2005, the criminal case went to trial in March of 2006, and the divorce trial transpired in the September of 2006.

Not long after Richard was released on bail, he returned to the cabinet business. I am persuaded he rented an apartment realizing a long journey lay ahead. Although he rented an apartment, I believe he continued to embrace the idea that we would reconcile at some future date. In retrospect, our previous history substantiated that I had always taken him back. My actions, from the beginning of our relationship, were like an old-timey LP record that got stuck while it was going around and around. I enthroned him and took him back no matter what he had done to me. Many of the letters that he wrote in the months following the felony charges were indicative of that mindset. I understood his perception as I had, for over 40 years, put him above all else and stayed married to him amid the dysfunction and abuse. He persisted in that vein of thought for months. He balked on selling our five hundred-thousand-dollar house, as he thought I would do as I always had done and take him back. He failed to grasp that the previously locked prison gates of truth had been flung open. By the grace of God, I had given the key to the prison gates to King Jesus. There would be no more locked gates and no more hidden truth.

The letters that Richard sent to me and others during the following months demonstrated that he had not believed my final words that he could never be my husband again. Quotes of portions of letters from Richard corroborate, clarify, and broaden the scope of his guilt and state of mind after the unveiling of the horrific tragedy in our family. A quote from Richard's letter to me dated May 4, 2005, Wednesday morning:

> "No matter how you feel about me; No matter what you try to do to me. I will always love you—Because, now I see plainly how much I do love you—No court decree—No man can stop our marriage—only God. I will beg God the last day of my life to have you back in fellowship with me and be my close companion again."

The following is a note Richard wrote and left for me at the house when he went back to get some of his personal items:

> "Bettye I Love you. If God ever grants forgiveness from you to me please have me back. I love you—have always loved you & appreciate all that you have done for me. I am so sorry for all of this."

I decided to pack the contents of the house, to move from West Point, and to relocate to nearby Columbus, Mississippi. Residing in the West Point house made me feel as if Richard continued to exert his control over me. My attorney had secured monthly rent and living expenses for me; therefore, I was financially positioned to move. During the deposition, Richard complained about the house I rented, stating that it was too expensive. Still oblivious to the fact he was no longer making the decisions for me, he ranted that he should have been the one to have chosen the house since he was the one that paid the rent. We remained in that first rent house until the criminal trial concluded.

After I made the decision to move to Columbus, Richard agreed to the sale of the West Point house. He, however, stipulated that he wanted in his possession a long list of furniture and household items in conjunction with his agreement to the sale of the house. When I moved from the West Point house, I left the bulk of the items he had demanded at the house. (All the items he had designated on his list were awarded to me in the final divorce settlement.) The West Point house sold not long after I moved. Each of us received less than $350 from the sale of the five hundred-thousand-dollar house, because a second mortgage that had been appropriated for the cabinet business had to be paid. I signed my $350 check to my attorney as a payment on my accelerating divorce debt.

Amid the preparation for the divorce trial, legal proceedings went forward for Richard's criminal trial. The amount of time that transpired from the revelation of the molestation to the criminal trial date was about a year. Our daughter Ruth was about four weeks from completing her junior year at college when the criminal trial preparation ramped up. She was so emotionally distraught, during this time, that she was unable to function with her college work. She, later, recounted how she went to class, sat, and stared into space. Before I realized what had happened, she had withdrawn from college. The mental trauma had culminated in a devastating blow to my sweet Ruth. Mental and emotional preparation for the criminal trial was extremely difficult for the girls and me. I also had the responsibility of preparing for the divorce trial by attending hearings, depositions, and answering detailed questions on lengthy documents.

A lot of buzz and local gossip circulated in the small Southern town concerning who was representing Richard in both the divorce case and the criminal case. I was told by various people that Richard had hired the best defense lawyers in our area. Originally, he had secured a West Point attorney for his criminal trial and a separate West Point attorney to handle the divorce. Both West Point attorneys were replaced after they had agreed to represent him. Richard retained two attorneys from Columbus, Mississippi, who were partners in a law firm. One focused on the divorce proceedings, and the other one took the lead in the criminal defense. I heard people from Columbus comment that his attorneys were fine men, and they applauded them as highly qualified, successful attorneys.

To represent a pedophile was beyond my understanding. Defending someone that hurt his children was just unfathomable to me. I heard statements like everyone deserved a good defense and representation. These men had been privy to Richard's statement of guilt he gave at the time of his arrest. So, how did these *fine* men operate on the premise that everyone deserved a good defense until proven guilty? They had secured firsthand knowledge of his guilt, in his words and from his mouth through copies of his statements to law enforcement. If one is interested in representing a confessed pedophile, let that be someone without scruples and standards. How can one with a moral code present a defense for one who has already confessed to pedophiliac crimes against his children? Well, in this life, men may comfort themselves with the persona of upholding justice and the rights of others; it is their choice. Eternity will reveal how men's comfort fares when standing before the Judge of all the earth. Oh, the foolish thoughts of men. The Bible states in the book of Proverbs there is a way that seems right to a man, but the end is the way of death. Remember, the heart is deceitful and desperately wicked, and who knows just how wicked?

Men deceive themselves to justify their actions. Some attorneys are sincerely interested in justice when defending clients. Other attorneys are interested in their clients' pocketbook. Attorneys portraying that they are acting in lieu of upholding justice and preserving men's rights when they have been motivated by financial gain should not, from my viewpoint, defend the pedophile who has confessed his guilt. I propose to let those who lay no claim on Christ or His gospel, if they so desire, defend the confessed pedophile in the interest that all deserve representation.

I experienced the actions of one of Richard's esteemed attorneys during one of the divorce depositions. His interrogation of me displayed, in my estimation, moments of sarcasm and egotism. I did not believe his actions paralleled the reputation that preceded him. If this attorney thought that he would provoke me to cower and be that former helpless abuse victim, he certainly had an awakening that day. I had been undergirded and empowered by my advocate, Jesus Christ the Righteous, and He was the only reason for my unmovable, strong spirit in my attorney's conference room as I faced the adversary. Christ had stood with me as I confronted Richard on the day of his initial confession, and He proved to be my sure and strong defense during the depositions.

Let me set the stage for you, my audience: I believe, if God had pulled back the curtain for our physical eyes to have seen the spiritual proponents in that conference room, we would all have been on the floor. Some may have been crumpled in great fear, while some of us would have had our hands stretched forth to Him in praise. I was not contending with men that day in the conference room, but I was wrestling against evil forces that were battling the righteous. God was not caught off guard by a surprise attack, and He would not suffer defeat. I clearly perceived demonic forces were in battle with the righteous that day on Broad Street in West Point, Mississippi, at the law firm of my attorney.

> *For we wrestle not against flesh and blood,*
> *but against principalities, against powers,*
> *against the rulers of the darkness of this*
> *world, against spiritual wickedness*
> *in high places. (Ephesians 6:12 KJV).*

> *... Be not afraid nor dismayed by reason of*
> *this great multitude; for the battle is not*
> *yours, but God's (II Chronicles 20:15 KJV).*

As the opposing attorney ridiculed and taunted me that day, God continued to hold me up as His little child. The scripture states:

> *But whoso shall offend one of these little ones*
> *which believe in me, it were better for him*
> *that a millstone were hanged about his neck,*
> *and that he were drowned in depth of the sea*
> *(Matthew 18: 6 KJV).*

As the State of Mississippi and the defense prepared their cases for the criminal trial, my daughters, other family members, and I leaned heavily on the Lord to get us through the impending event. Although our lives had been forever altered, we found ourselves muddling through the ordinary functions of our daily routine. Our hearts and the very core of who we were had been accosted by the roaring lion seeking to devour us. We felt the intense fires of the forces of evil as we stood our ground for truth. Many times, precious saints of God would come along beside me and offer consolation and comfort through fellowship, financial support, and the compassion spoken about in the epistle of Colossians. My spiritual family ministered multiple acts of kindness, which sometimes had been simply a warm, sincere smile or embrace. Love is a powerful and mighty balm to administer unto God's children as the blessed Holy Spirit directs. My heart recorded each act of pure love shared with me during that traumatic time. God placed some of His precious children around me to care for me and hold me up, and He took note of their love and compassion they shared with His wounded child.

> *For God is not unrighteous to forget your work and labor of love, which ye have shown toward his name, in that ye have ministered to the saints, and do minister (Hebrews 6: 10 KJV).*

When the Circuit Court of Noxubee County, Mississippi, convened for its regularly scheduled March term in 2006, State of Mississippi v. Vaden, No. 2005-031 (Noxubee Cty. Circuit Ct. 2006) was on the court docket to be heard by the presiding Honorable Lee J. Howard, Circuit Judge. My daughters Rachel, Ruth, Mary, and I were scheduled to testify. We were joined by my oldest daughter, Amy, who drove from Wisconsin, through a scary snowstorm, to support us. Jake my son (Jacob Benjamin) was also in attendance to support us. Two of Richard's cousins, who I loved and had known for years, had driven from Tennessee to support us. Carol brought MeMa, Richard's and her elderly mother to the trial. She was so frail, and I was told that she could be seen nodding off to sleep sometimes as the trial was in session. My heart broke for her that she was subjected to this most difficult time. I did not know who had made the decision for her to attend, but she was there each day. When the grandchildren tried to speak to their grandmother in the courthouse hallway, Carol, Richard's sister, objected.

One of Richard's cousins, who grew up with me, was at the trial, along with her sister. We attended the same school our first nine years and had gone to church together in Cottage Grove, Tennessee. I called her soon after I learned of the molestation, and we kept in close contact from that time until the trial. Furthermore, I was encouraged and supported by most of Richard's family. Since Richard and I had been married over forty years, I certainly was not a stranger to them. The family knew when I left Richard and took legal action that I had spoken the truth about him molesting the girls. One of Richard's cousins wrote and warned me to be prudent about my safety until he was convicted and incarcerated.

In digression, I called Richard's sister while he was held in one of the county jails. I conveyed that Richard had molested the girls. Since I was speaking the truth, I anticipated she would believe me. I was naive about that assumption. It was not long before it became evident that both Richard's sister and her husband were on the band wagon for the defense and saving of Richard Vaden. Moreover, during the second phone call, Carol's husband did the talking, but he related to me that Carol could hear the conversation. I questioned him about where they stood with their support. My words were direct and without hesitation as I candidly asked whom they supported. There was no pretense with me. The lines of the coming battles of whom would be supporting whom had been drawn, evidently earlier for them. For me, it was that day, that phone call that confirmed that the two of them had sold out truth. I did not know if they sold out because of family, prospect of money, or some other hidden agenda.

Carol traveled to Mississippi from Georgia on two occasions after learning of the charges against Richard. She aspired to convince some of our family that Richard was innocent. Her first appearance was at my daughter Amy's house. I was alerted that she had come, so I immediately headed to Amy's. Carol pleaded with John, Amy, and me during her visit for us to love and forgive Richard. She declared Richard's innocence during her appeal. I wondered with that mind set why she told us we needed to forgive him, if according to her, he had not committed the abuse? Her attempts to change our minds that day were unsuccessful, in fact, we had already declared the truth to law enforcement.

Her last-ditch effort played out at my West Point house. She and her husband Bob appeared, unannounced, at my door, one day. Carol counseled me to drop the charges against Richard. In an attempt to influence me, she related a story from years ago when she said that she had been molested by a family member. Per her testimony, the incident was never reported to law enforcement, and both she and her abuser had lived productive, normal lives. Why did Carol interject her story of molestation since she said Richard was innocent? Her position was for us to refrain from doing anything to Richard. As in her previous visit to Amy's, she continued to lobby the aspect of forgiving Richard. Her strategy of appeal was baffling to me. Why did this woman keep emphasizing our need to forgive her brother and to move forward like nothing had happened when at the same time, she defended his innocence? Her platform of pleas and bargains was ambiguous and faulty to me. She promised he would never bother us or try to contact us if we would just drop the charges.

A declaration of Richard's profound love for me was also expressed by Carol during her visit. His realization of just how much he loved and needed me was part of the message Richard's sister was peddling during that encounter. She said she had a letter from him for me that day. She, however, did not leave the letter remarking that I might use it against him. I was not swayed by her tears or drama to alter my position of upholding the truth. The girls and I were committed to telling the truth. Our choices were at opposite ends of the poles. I told Carol, as she sat in my living room, that she had a choice, and, evidently, she had made her choice to defend Richard. We had chosen truth and had made our statements to law enforcement.

During my long marriage to Richard, it was evident to me that he and his sister did not characterize a harmonious relationship. After Richard's Bible doctrine became narrow, I witnessed the many times that hurtful words were exchanged between them. Richard spoke harshly to his sister and mother concerning his doctrine or their response to his doctrine. I observed their already strained compatibility deteriorate. It became increasingly difficult for Richard and his sister to converse without reciprocating with angry and wounding words.

To witness the complete turnaround between Richard and Carol was monumental to me. From a difficult and strained relationship as siblings in the past years, they had transitioned to sympathetic, supportive roles. The metamorphosis of their relationship emerged following the revelation of the girls' molestation by Richard and was astounding to me. You know, I had not just fallen off the cabbage truck, to echo a colloquial saying. I had been married to the man for over 40 years and had witnessed firsthand their fiery, pernicious exchanges. Another facet of their prior shaky relationship was Richard's private words to me concerning his sister. He often made fun of her in front of our children and condemned her marriage to her second husband, because she had divorced husband number one. Her husband at the time of the criminal trial was husband number three. Despite all the history they had experienced over the years, Carol became her brother's ally and number one defender.

Evidence and Exposure

My heart raced, and fear gripped my being as I was signaled to the courtroom. It was Tuesday, the second day of the trial when my appointed time to testify arrived. I was designated as a hostile witness for the defense. No one explained to me the concept of a hostile witness, so I was unaware of the defense team's strategy as I entered the courtroom. Richard's attorneys planned an attempt to discredit my integrity and impeach me. A hostile witness position for the defense meant the witness was directly opposed to the defense's case. Since I was assigned as a hostile defense witness, Richard's attorney could ask me leading questions. He could use both direct-examination and cross-examination while questioning me. The defense attorneys had planned an attempt to establish a contradiction in my trial testimony with statements I had made prior to the trial or during trial. It was only after the trial concluded that I understood what the defense had intended to assert. The Lord harnessed my fear and trepidation level during my time of testimony due to my lack of understanding of the defense's strategy.

My legs trembled as I walked into the courtroom and advanced toward the witness box. I was sworn in by the court official and took my seat. Once the sound waves that carried the first question connected with my hearing mechanism, the peace of God flooded my heart and mind. I knew He was present and in charge. I concentrated, without distraction, on what the attorney asked me. The only instruction any of us had prior to the trial was just tell the *truth.*

While on the witness stand, I often felt badgered by Richard's attorney. Following my answers, he sometimes rolled his eyes at me. Occasionally, he made what I considered inflammatory remarks. From time-to-time, the attorney made statements instead of asking me questions. I think he was trying to intimidate me and cause me to stumble and error. I listened carefully to the way he phrased his statements and questions, for it seemed to me that he endeavored to entrap me and cause me to agree with false statements. A portion of what he said could be accurate, but he would sometimes include information with which I did not agree.

Portions of my (Betty Vaden) testimony during the trial of the State of Mississippi v. Vaden, No. 2005-031 (Noxubee Cty. Circuit Ct. 2006). will appear in this chapter. The following notations clarify the speakers during my testimony.

A: Betty Vaden

Q: Defense Attorney, Mr. Ray

By The Court: Honorable Judge Lee J. Howard

MS. Patricia Faver: Prosecutor from District Attorney's Office

By The Witness: Betty Vaden

I made references during my testimony to some of Richard's dictates he had preached over the years, which one of the local newspapers reported in a summarized form. More importantly than a newspaper, I believed my words were recorded in the pages of God's legal journal in His halls of justice. My words indicated the depth of some of the weighty chains from which God had delivered me. One instance, Mr. Ray had questioned me about the control Richard exerted over me. The newspaper article summarized my words indicating that I had been taught through Richard Vaden's preaching that I could only please God through my husband. The article inferred that I had now found liberty and no longer had to please God by pleasing Richard Vaden. I said in my testimony that, "I had found a liberty that I can worship God now without him telling me how to do it."

The following is a portion of my (Betty Vaden) testimony in the jury trial of the State of Mississippi v. Vaden, No. 2005-031 (Noxubee Cty. Circuit Ct. 2006).

"Q. Isn't it correct that it was a decision by you and your husband to homeschool your children and teach them yourselves?
A. Richard Vaden made the decision for the household.
Q. Was he a dominating influence in the house?
A. He was a dominating influence in the house.
Q. Did you appreciate that domination?
A. (No response.)
Q. Did you like it?
A. There could be - - I did not like the control that he exerted when it was abusive.
Q. Okay. Isn't it true that you in fact resented that control?
A. No, sir. That is not true.
Q. You did not resent the control?
A. That is not true. The resentment is not a word that I would choose. I was saddened. I was hurt. And I was embarrassed many times by his abuse.
Q. Did that abuse, as you phrase it, cause problems between you and your husband?
A. The abuse itself is a problem.
Q. That's what I'm asking. Did that - -
A. Abuse is - - yes, sir. Abuse I would consider a problem.
Q. Did that cause the marital relationship to be strained with regard to the way y'all acted with each other?
A. I was trying to please God, Mr. Ray, according to the dictates that I had heard preached. My goal was to please God." (Tr. at 312:1-29).

At times, the defense attorney failed to follow procedure and made statements instead of asking questions of me. My (Betty Vaden) following testimony will show his incorrect procedure.

"Q. Mrs. Vaden, you can answer questions of what you observed and give general consensus of what was going on in your family, can't you, because you gave one about Ruth?

MS. FAVER: Your Honor, I don't believe that's a question. I'm going to object.

BY THE COURT: Sustained.

Q. A while ago, Mrs. Vaden, I was asking you questions about children having friends and doing things outside the house, and you said you'd have to ask specifically. I'm asking for a general - -

BY THE COURT: Let's cross–examine, please, and ask questions and not make statements.

BY MR. RAY: I apologize, Your Honor.

BY THE COURT: Ask questions of the witness." (Tr. at 313:26-314:11).

During my testimony, Mr. Ray questioned me about the cabinet business Richard owned.

"Q. When the allegations were made by Rachel, Ruth, and Mary, isn't it true, Mrs. Vaden, that you and John, and Butch Barriff took over the business?

A. I never took over any business.

Q. You did not instruct your son John - -

A. I never - - excuse me. Go ahead and finish.

Q. - - to take the business over and not let your husband come back on the property?

A. No, sir.

Q. You want the business to keep going though, don't you?

A. That is not my primary interest.

Q. Your interest - - you don't have an interest that Triangle Cabinetry keep going?

A. My interest is my children.

Q. You don't have an interest that Triangle Cabinetry keep making money and providing for you?

A. My primary interest is in the welfare of my children." (Tr. at 316:27-317:16).

From time to time, the defense attorney did not follow procedure and sometimes asked improper questions of me. The following quotes from two portions of my testimony give examples of those improper procedures and questions by the defense attorney.

"Q. Have you discussed your testimony in preparation for testifying with anybody?

A. Sir?

Q. Who have you discussed your testimony with?

BY THE COURT: I gave you some latitude as to cross-examination, Counsel. That does not mean that she is still not your witness.

BY MR. RAY: I believe the rules allow me to impeach my own witness's credibility, Your Honor, even if she's my own witness.

BY THE COURT: That's not what you're doing, Counsel. We're going back to direct examination in just a moment if you continue questioning as you did the last question." (Tr. at 318:4-17).

"Q. Isn't it true, Mrs. Vaden, that you hired attorneys for Rachel and Ruth to keep them from having to go to a deposition with regard to your divorce?

BY MS. FAVER: Your Honor, I'm going to object again.

BY THE COURT: The objection is sustained.

BY MR. RAY: Your Honor, may I not - -

BY THE COURT: The objection is sustained.

BY MR. RAY: Well, I would like the Court's direction as to my further questions to avoid having to ask improper questions.

BY THE COURT: You called the witness. The objection, however, is sustained.

BY MR. Ray: All right." (Tr. at 318:26-319:10).

During my testimony, Richard's attorney questioned me about our lifestyle during the days we had lived a very isolated life while residing in Aberdeen, Mississippi. Then he asked me if we lived the same way after we moved to West Point. Quote from my (Betty Vaden) testimony during the trial:

"Q. And, in particular, for a length of time, your family was very strict about not watching TV, not wearing certain types of clothes; is that true?

A. When we lived in Aberdeen, Mississippi.

Q. Was it like that when you lived in West Point?

A. No, sir. When Rebecca Davis died, it changed.

BY MR. RAY: Your Honor, I need to bring something to the Court's attention outside the presence of the jury in the form of a motion." (Tr. at 325:20-28).

The Judge instructed the court officer to usher the jury from the courtroom. My heart seemed to practically pound out of my chest in that moment. I imagined that I had caused a mistrial, but the reason, I had not understood. The jury was escorted from the courtroom. In the absence of the jury, Mr. Ray continued to speak to the Judge.

"BY MR. RAY: Comes now the defendant, Your Honor, makes a motion in limine to ask the Court to instruct this witness not to make any mention or testify with regard to anything having to do with a specific allegation of a criminal act by my client in Aberdeen, Mississippi, for which he was nonadjudicated. His record was expunged. This witness I feel is about to testify about that, and I'm asking the Court in limine to instruct her not to talk about the specific act that we're aware of and that everybody's aware of in this case. It's not relevant, and it's not admissible under the rules of evidence. That was nonresponsive to my answer - - I mean, excuse me, to my question. It's obvious that this witness wants to testify about that.

BY THE COURT: I haven't gotten that yet out of the witness's testimony by what she has said. You stood. You have something you want to add to this?

BY MS. FAVER: She responded to his question. She said after this child died, everything in their house changed. The way they acted. The way their religion was. She was responsive to his question. The Court is not aware of what I believe Mr. Ray is talking about.

BY THE COURT: Haven't got the faintest idea.

BY MS. FAVER: Exactly. For the Court to instruct otherwise, I think you need to be brought up to date. She answered his question. Isn't it not true that your religion was such a way and she said, no, it changed after Rebecca Davis died. This jury has no idea who Rebecca Davis is nor does this Court. She's a child that died as a result of his religious beliefs in Monroe County and he was charged with it.

BY THE COURT: That may be an unfair statement that you just made.

BY MS. FAVER: Outside the presence -- I'm trying to explain to the Court.

BY THE COURT: I think I understand what you're getting to.

BY MR. RAY: Your Honor, I just didn't - - I felt she was about to say something that's highly prejudicial. I'm just trying to head it off without it being said in front of the jury.

BY THE COURT: You're right. I didn't know anything about it. I don't know who Rebecca Davis is or was or anything about it. But anything that happened that precedes the events that we're on trial about, I think probably ought not to be gone into. And I would so instruct the witness. You understand what I just said?

BY THE WITNESS: Yes, sir. I just don't know how to answer.

BY THE COURT: You have already answered the question.

BY THE WITNESS: If he proceeds on because things did change.

BY THE COURT: Now, you are having great latitude in questioning the witness.

BY MR. RAY: I understand, Your Honor.

BY THE COURT: And I think that that latitude so far is justified, but you must also be aware that you called the witness. You may get stuck with the answer.

BY MR. RAY: I understand that, Your Honor.

BY THE COURT: Show the jury back in, please." (Tr. at 326:4-328:13).

The following excerpt from the transcript of my testimony demonstrates some of the control Richard had exerted and revealed a heavy chain from which I had been delivered.

"Q. Did he make the decision about whether your clothes were appropriate?

A. He didn't go shopping with me all the time, no.

Q. He didn't tell you what you could or couldn't wear, did he?

A. If I'd worn something he did not approve of he would have told me, yes.

Q. And would you have stopped wearing that?

A. Sir?

Q. Would you have changed if he told you not to wear something?

A. Yes, sir.

Q. You didn't like that, did you?

A. I wanted to please God. And he taught me that I could only do that through my husband.

Q. And that's part of the control that you've testified about earlier?

A. Yes, sir, He controlled us religiously.

Q. You don't like that - - didn't like that, did you?

A. I have found a liberty that I can worship God now without him telling me how to do it." (Tr. at 329:15-330:6).

When I was questioned by the defense attorney, I felt that sometimes he seemed confused. At one point during my testimony, the Judge ordered Mr. Ray, the defense attorney, not to argue with me about my answer. The following is a portion of my testimony which illustrates that the defense counsel refuted my answer.

"Q. And you testified that you were around his family, correct? His mama and daddy? Were you around his sister, Carol?

A. Carol never lived where we did.

Q. Y'all were friends, were you not?

A. I didn't really know Carol until his mother started getting older.

Q. You didn't know your sister-in-law that you were - -

A. No, sir. I didn't never live with her.

Q. You were married to her brother for 41 years and you never knew her?

BY THE COURT: Counsel, let's not argue with the answer that she gives when she does give an answer.
BY MR. RAY: Yes, sir." (Tr. at (332:7-22).

    My three girls were covered with God's sweet protection as He ministered strength and boldness to them during their testimony. Each girl was called separately to the witness box, questioned by Richard's attorneys, and questioned by the state prosecutor. They spoke about the details of their molestation in front of the attorneys, the judge, the jury, all the court officers, and all who were present to witness the trial proceedings. My daughters faced their violator who was their daddy and testified about his sexual abuse to them in his presence.

    The girls related somewhat of a similar experience during their testimonies as I had with the defense attorney in my testimony. One of the girls said that the attorney questioning her became confused as to which daughter she was and called the wrong daughter's name. Richard's attorneys failed to substantiate the precedent and theory they had initially claimed that the evidence was going to support. In my (Betty Vaden) testimony in the State of Mississippi v. Vaden, No. 2005-031 (Noxubee Cty. Circuit Ct. 2006) the defense attorney Mr. Ray said: "It's relevant because evidence is going to show that this lady and the family wanted to take over the business, and that's one of the reasons these allegations were made. I said that in my opening statement." (Tr. at 315:13-17). The trial scenario, to me, bore resemblance to a battle from the pages of the Old Testament where God confused the enemy and they slaughtered one another. God was ruling in that courtroom. From my experience on the witness stand, I sensed confusion and frustration from the defense attorney, and I thought that this trial was probably not his nor his partner's finest hour.

The state prosecutor for the case was a young woman, who presented herself professionally. During the time I was present in the courtroom, she did not fumble for names or get confused with her presentation. She was well prepared. The prosecutor had gained the trust of the girls and performed her job proficiently as the state's assistant district attorney during Richard's trial. She followed the correct procedures and demonstrated competence as she performed within the scope of the duties of her position. Richard taught and practiced the ideology that a woman should not hold or execute a place of authority in any realm. I wondered how a female serving as the prosecuting attorney, during his trial, had gone for him. After the trial, the prosecutor related to us that at one time during her questioning of Richard, she approached the Judge and spoke to him, calling him, "Your Honor." Richard answered her as if she were addressing him instead of the Judge. She said the courtroom became excruciatingly quiet.

All the witnesses were permitted to be present in the courtroom as the defense attorneys and the prosecution laid out the closing arguments. On one hand during their closing, the defense team proclaimed Richard's innocence. Then they adversely injected that Richard had thought he was confessing only to a misdemeanor. *Oh my!* Now the defense said he had confessed. Big swing of the pendulum, I would say. He confessed, but should not be held accountable for a felony because he thought what he had done was only a little bad? Please forgive me, but why did it matter whether he thought the crime he had confessed was a misdemeanor? The lawful level of his deeds, whether a misdemeanor or a felony, did not eradicate his own words of guilt.

The following is a portion of the closing statement in State of Mississippi v. Vaden No. 2005-031 (Noxubee Cty. Circuit Ct.

2006). presented by defense attorney Rod Ray as he defended what his client Richard Vaden confessed to Deputy Sheriff, Billy Perkins:

" ... I didn't know what fondling meant. I saw something on TV when I was working out that a policeman in Columbus was accused of misdemeanor fondling with six girls. I didn't know what fondling was. I didn't know it was a crime where they're going to slam the book and say book him. ... " (Tr. at 549:17-22).

In the State of Mississippi v. Vaden, the prosecution presented the following portion of the closing arguments:

" ...when those three girls came to her and said Daddy has been doing this to us, and she confronted him and as guts and arrogant as he is, he turned around to her and said, yeah, I did it. Yep, I did it. But laughed in her face basically and said what are you going to do about it? You've been with me for 40 years. I been doing a lot of things for 40 years. You know what? Finally she stood up. You can treat me badly. You can do this to me. But you did it to my girls. And that's why we're here. Not because of the business. Not because of the money. But because of what he did to these girls year after year after year in Clay County and here in Noxubee County at that river house that he bought and shoved down their throat every chance he got. Look what I give you, look what I give you. You're ungrateful. Nobody appreciates me. Took the stand. I work every day 12 hours a day. Told you over and over again how great he is, and that's what he told them. And every day he reinforced do not go against me or you will reap the repercussions.

And finally, yesterday on the stand he admitted it. No, I didn't teach them that. I didn't preach them that. Until it was in his own writing and I had to show it to him. All the way up to July 2005, his 40-year-old son he was still doing it. Remember that time you went against me? Yeah, he went against his father. He beat his father up. I finally got him to admit it. In less than a month he had a car accident and almost died. What does this man tell him? That's God punishing you because you went against me. And then in 2005 what does he do? He puts it in writing again. You remember. You stand by me. You get your mother to drop these charges. You get those girls to do what they're supposed to do. And you remember what happened the last time you went against the man of God. You vividly remember those consequences. Because that is what he did. And that is how he kept them in line.

He keeps saying these girls are making it up. They did not. He didn't do any of these things. You know why? They didn't make this up. These are his words and what he said.

(WHEREUPON THE EXHIBIT WAS PLAYED IN OPEN
COURT.)
BY MS. FAVER: His words." (Tr. at 530:24-532:14).

The most convincing and weighty evidence presented in the entire trial, apart from the girls' testimonies, was the recording of the taped interview on April 16, 2005, of Richard Vaden by Mr. Billy Perkins, Deputy Sheriff, Clay County Sheriff's Department in West Point, Mississippi. This taped confession was played in the courtroom during the closing arguments in the State of Mississippi v. Vaden, after which the prosecutor so aptly stated, "His words." (Tr. at 532:14). He had been read his Miranda rights which he had signed. He was advised that allegations of the molestation of three of his daughters had been made. Then Richard, by his own mouth and in his own words, confessed his guilt to Mr. Perkins. From the taped statement, Richard was heard admitting guilt to some of the incidents of the sexual abuse. It is almost inconceivable that a father would do those things to his daughters. He told places we lived when it had happened. He confessed that he was sorry and told one of the girls that he would not do it again. He confessed that it was sick, that it was embarrassing to talk about, and that he was ashamed of it.

The condemning evidence of Richard's taped confession given to law enforcement and presented by the State in the closing arguments was overwhelmingly compelling. The State spoke in the first segment in the closing argument portion. In the next segment, the Defense presented their first portion of their closing arguments as Mr. Ford, defense attorney, spoke. The trial recessed after Mr. Ford finished. Following the recess, the jury was called back to the Court. The Defense resumed its closing arguments, and Mr. Ray, defense attorney, spoke in the defense's concluding segment on behalf of his client Richard Vaden. The final portion of the closing arguments was by the State and the prosecuting attorney, Ms. Faver. When the State finished that final segment of closing arguments, the jury was excused to deliberate, and we went back to the witness room to await the verdict. After the jury had deliberated a few hours, we were told to return to the Court for the jury's verdict.

The jury was composed of Everlena Glenn and eleven others, who had each been approved by both sides. After they had heard the evidence, the argument of counsel, and received the Court's instructions, they retired to consider the evidence presented and to decide a verdict. This jury returned to the Open Court and declared the Defendant guilty as charged in Count 1, guilty as charged in Count 2, and not guilty as charged in Count 3.

My girls, other family members, and I were present when the verdict was handed down in the courtroom. We had been instructed not to show our emotions or display any kind of visible outburst of our thoughts and feelings. The family appeared as statues and refrained from any visible signs of emotion. Richard was directed, as is customary, to stand facing the Judge while his verdict was read. He stood motionless and void of any expression. On the other side of the courtroom, however, the distinct wailing and pretentious display of the words of his sister could be heard in the entire courtroom when his verdict was handed down.

As Richard was taken from the Noxubee County Courthouse in hand cuffs, he smiled and spoke to bystanders. He continued to play the blame game instead of accepting responsibility for his depraved actions. As he talked to people outside the courthouse, he told them that we would have to live with what we had done. His statement to the bystanders was spot on and completely in character for him.

The trial began on Monday, March 20, 2006. Within a few days, I believe on Thursday, we were directed to return to the Noxubee County Court House to hear the sentencing of Richard. His attorney was present in the court room with him as he faced the indictment charging him with the crime of Fondling §97-5-23. He had previously entered a not guilty plea. He stood facing the girls, John, Amy, me, and other family members who had gathered in the courtroom. He was sentenced on March 23, 2006, which was his sixtieth birthday. Judge Lee J. Howard sentenced him to Ten (10) years in the Mississippi Department of Corrections for each of the two counts he was found guilty, required him to pay all costs of the Court, and required him to pay the fine in the amount of $1000.00 for each count. The sentence was to run concurrently for each of the two counts for which he was convicted in Noxubee County Circuit Court Cause #2005-031. Count #1 and Count #2. Upon his release from confinement, Richard was ordered to register as a sex offender pursuant to the state statute.

Many convicted criminals' attorneys immediately file necessary paperwork to appeal the conviction of their client. The convicted criminals (I do not know if there are stipulations regarding the type of crime committed before one is eligible to file said motion.) can then file a motion for bond pending the appeal. This translates that they possibly could be awarded a get-out-of-jail free card while their conviction awaits an appeal if the presiding judge so rules.

The prosecuting attorney discouraged us as to the outcome of the bail bond hearing. Her thoughts were that Judge Howard would grant the bail bond pending appeal for Richard. She instructed us that we had the right, as victims, to author letters stating why we thought Richard Vaden should be denied bail pending the appeal. Several of the family composed letters substantiating the reasons we were convinced that his bond pending appeal should be denied.

If the Judge approved the bail bond, that meant that Richard could avoid incarceration until the decision of the Court of Appeals of Mississippi was decided. Our family was both fearful and frustrated that he could possibly walk free for a time. He was a confessed, convicted pedophile. If the Judge ruled to grant the bail bond pending appeal, he would have opportunity to harm or harass those who had spoken truth about the charges he had faced. Our letters were penned and delegated to Judge Howard to consider. The prosecutor reminded us that the decision of the Judge to deny bail pending the appeal did not look favorable for us. Richard was held in the local Noxubee County Jail until the Judge ruled on the motion for the bail bond.

This Court Order, which ruled on the Defendant's Motion For Bond Pending Appeal, is included in the case file of the State of Mississippi v. Vaden, No. 2005-031 (Noxubee Cty. Circuit Ct.

2006). This order was ruled on April 25, 2006, by the Honorable Judge Lee Howard and is presented below:

State of Mississippi v. Richard Vaden

ORDER

This cause having come on to be heard on the Defendant's Motion for Bond Pending Appeal, and the Court having heard the parties, does here find as follows:

I.

Pursuant to § 99-35-115 of the Mississippi Code of 1972, letters from the victims in this matter have been admitted into evidence for purposes of this bail pending appeal and have been considered by the Court. The Court has considered that the victims in this case do not want the Defendant released while his case is pending appeal.

II.

The Defendant has failed to show by clear and convincing evidence that his release would not constitute a special danger to the victims as required by § 99-35-115(2)(a) of the Mississippi Code of 1972

III.

Based on the evidence heard during the trial and the testimony at this hearing, the Court further finds that the Defendant poses a great risk to the safety and welfare of the victims in this case. WHEREFORE, PREMISES CONSIDERED, the Court hereby finds that the Defendant's Motion for Bail Pending Appeal should be and is hereby denied.

SO ORDERED, this 25th day of April, 2006.

We were thankful that the Lord defended us in the hearing (we were not present), and that we could breathe without fear and anxiety. The decision of Richard's appeal was handed down May 8, 2007, by the higher Mississippi Court. It was affirmative action on our behalf. The Court of Appeals of Mississippi disallowed that all the arguments presented by Richard's attorneys were without merit and that there was no cumulative error that would necessitate reversal; therefore, the appeals court affirmed the lower court's decision.

Sometime after Richard's incarceration to Mississippi Department of Corrections, maybe within the first year, the charges in Clay County, Mississippi, went before the Grand Jury. The courthouse for Clay County was in our hometown of West Point. I went with Ruth when she was called to testify at the Grand Jury hearing. Of course, I was not allowed to be in the Grand Jury room with her. It was an extremely difficult day for her. She told me she broke down and cried as she gave her testimony, and that some of the members of the Grand Jury also cried. When she came back into the room where I was waiting, her countenance was downcast. She wept as she asked why this had happened to her, but she added that she realized it had made her the person she was. She was the only daughter that had been molested in Clay County; thus, the only one presented before the Grand Jury that day. Richard was once again indicted on felony charges.

When the Clay County District Circuit Court convened for one of the regular scheduled court terms, Richard's case was on the docket. There was a rape case that was scheduled to be heard ahead of us. My girls, Jacob, and I waited our turn for our case to be heard. We watched law enforcement escort a cuffed and shackled Richard Vaden, with his defense attorney trailing behind, down the hallway adjoining the room where we waited. Ultimately, the rape case took so long that we were told there would not be enough time in that court term to proceed with our case.

Later, the assistant district attorney, who tried the earlier case in Noxubee County, contacted Ruth about going forward with the Clay County case in the next court term. She told Ruth it would be up to her whether the state went forward with the Clay County indictment, since she was the only victim in that case. Ruth decided not to go forward with the second trial in the next term of Circuit Court for Clay County; hence, the case was retired to the file. Emotionally, Ruth had been devastated by the events of the molestation during her life, and a trial was like reliving those traumatic events. She suffered all the years the molestation occurred, she suffered during the unveiling of the molestation, she suffered during the preparation for the first trial, she suffered during the Noxubee County trial, and she suffered during the Clay County Grand Jury testimony. The emotional wounds were overwhelming for her. Since Richard was convicted, sentenced, and incarcerated as a result of the first trial, she decided not to go forward with a second trial which would have heaped additional trauma upon her.

Following the court proceedings, Richard's sister, Carol, came to Mississippi and remained in West Point for an extended time. Carol, with Richard's assistance by phone from jail, went forward with the cabinet business and continued to sign contracts for jobs. During the divorce proceedings a few months later, Richard claimed to have five hundred thousand dollars of signed contracts. Different negative accounts surfaced about the *goings on* at Triangle Cabinets. It was rumored that Triangle Cabinets had taken partial payments up-front from customers and never delivered the finished products unto them. Some of the taxes were not paid for the cabinet business, and the IRS shut down the business. An auction of the buildings' contents was orchestrated by the IRS to collect revenue for the delinquent taxes. The buildings and property reverted to the bank that held the mortgage.

The Divorce

I filed for divorce in the Chancery Court of Clay County, Mississippi, in April 2005. The divorce trial Cause No. 2005-0125 transpired in September of 2006 with Honorable Dorothy Colom Chancery Judge in West Point, Mississippi, presiding. The divorce was granted February 9, 2007. The court found that I had met the burden of proof required that entitled me to a divorce on the ground of habitual cruel and inhuman treatment and on the ground of Richard being sentenced to the penitentiary without being pardoned. The following explanation was presented in the final judgement of divorce: "habitual cruel and inhuman treatment can be conduct so unnatural and infamous as to make the marriage revolting to the unoffending spouse and render it impossible for that spouse to discharge the duties of marriage, thus destroying the basis for it continuing." **Potts v. Potts,** *700 So. 2d 321* (Miss. 1997). The final divorce judgement stated that Richard had spent at least $96, 700.00 for fees to his attorneys in his defense of the fondling charges and the divorce. I was awarded the following marital assets:

> Forty percent (40 %) of Vaco 1;
>
> Fifty percent (50 %) of R & B;
>
> The household furnishings;
>
> The Mississippi Farm Bureau Insurance Claim; and
>
> The Quail Ridge property.

Vaco 1 was the cabinet business and R& B held the deeds to the business real estate. The business Vaco 1 failed, and the contents of the buildings were confiscated and sold by IRS for delinquent taxes. The business real estate reverted to the bank that held the mortgage. The Farm Bureau Insurance Claim failed to proceed to trial; therefore, no settlement was reached or awarded. I signed over the Quail Ridge property to my divorce attorney. I was not financially able to maintain the taxes on this property, and the taxes were delinquent. Since the taxes were delinquent, the property was to be sold at a public auction. (About three years prior to signing the property to my attorney, he and his law firm forgave my remaining debt for the divorce.) I was awarded two thousand five hundred dollars a month for alimony and five hundred dollars a month for child support. I received one alimony check and one child support check total. The household furnishings was the only marital asset that I received when the divorce was finalized.

Mary visited Richard early in his imprisonment to confront him, one last time. She faced him with the truth of his actions of the sexual violations he committed unto her. He looked at her and denied his guilt. He kept eluding to some dark mystery in his family that was an underlying problem. She told him if he wanted to reveal anything to her that he needed to do it then, because it would probably be the last time, she would ever see him. He did not divulge any mystery, secret, or ask for forgiveness. Remember, when I talked to him on the morning of April 15, 2005, Richard asked me to get the girls together, so he could ask their forgiveness.

The testimony of our children who communicated with Richard following his incarceration has been that he has not changed, repented, or sought to seek forgiveness for his heinous actions of molestation to his daughters.

A lot of time elapsed before I was undergirded to face God about forgiving Richard. When I first grappled with forgiving him, I was afraid if I did forgive him that I would be obligated to resume my relationship with him. I knew I never could be his wife again, because of his licentious behavior to our daughters. However, I continued to seek God on the matter of forgiveness. I did come to rest in the promises of my heavenly Father. A better understanding of forgiveness and its purpose was revealed unto me. I learned that biblical forgiveness was not provided by God to reconcile relationships, and it was not provided to disregard the guilt or the accountability of the offending party. I have been commanded to forgive those who sin against God with reference to me. Forgiveness is between God and an individual. When that act transpires, the person is empowered by God to forgive others. Since I am a sinner who needs forgiveness, I should be willing to forgive others. God provided an avenue whereby I could unload my burden, and I had assumed the load of not forgiving. Failing to move forward and forgive Richard was not scriptural; therefore, it was not beneficial. Forgiveness is a direct command of God. If we have failed to forgive others, we remain in direct disobedience to God. Forgiveness is not impossible. God is not unjust or uncaring in commanding us to forgive, for forgiveness is freeing. Sometimes, we resist relinquishing our pride or pain to Him. Do not lug around your wounds like you are portraying a martyr, because unforgiveness is a weighty chain that could destroy. Get desperate with God. Beg for a heart change. Fast and pray for a desire to forgive. Yield unto Him, and He will deliver you. The blessed Holy Spirit, by His power, revealed to me the meaning as well as the application of forgiveness, and I forgave Richard. I was set free of a weighty chain and spared destruction from a root of bitterness.

After I forgave Richard, I refrained from telling anyone including him. God made it clear to me that I needed to write Richard and tell him that I forgave him. I did not let him off the hook of his accountability or his guilt. I told Richard that I prayed earnestly for him to forego his fleshly desires and the protective coat of armor that he had enshrouded around his heart and confess the truth as he had to me that night in his Tahoe. I told him that he knows the truth, I know the truth, the girls know the truth, and above all,

God knows the truth. I told him that he would be the loser if he did not confess. I said there is victory in truth and confession. I told him that I forgave him for his molestation of the girls, his inequities toward all our children, and his unfaithfulness and inequities to me. I told him I could forgive him because the Lord had done a work in my heart. I told him that I prayed that he would be released from the great bondage of self-preservation and the fear of his own condemnation. I said with Him all things are possible and without Him destruction awaits. I said I prayed for him to find the peace that passes all comprehension, and that grace and mercy would be granted unto him. I am sure he will share with his family, and those he has injured emotionally and spiritually when he is brought to repentance and confession. May God's will be done on earth as it is in Heaven. Amen.

Epilogue

Richard Vaden was released from prison March 20, 2016 and is a registered sex offender pursuant to the statutes of the State of Mississippi.

The journey of life has continued with victories and struggles for my family. Richard's failure to provide the court ordered alimony and child support deemed it necessary for me to join the workforce at age 59. I had not performed in the public workplace for more than thirty years. Employers were not interested in a nearly sixty-year-old woman employee with references and work experience that were some thirty years prior. I was rejected in all my attempts to gain employment, including the fast-food business. To earn money, I cleaned personal homes and a few businesses. Richard's failure to maintain the car payment on the Suburban I drove at the time of my family tragedy resulted in its repossession. Without a vehicle, I resorted to walking to the places I cleaned. For a couple of months, I walked to church, the grocery, or wherever I went unless someone offered me a ride. A couple of months later I fell and suffered a back fracture. After my recovery, I was physically unable to maintain the cleaning work.

Through the kindness and mercy of my heavenly Father, I secured a position in an office about six months later. A dear friend who was a sister in Christ was instrumental in locating this avenue of work for me. My heart rejoiced to have a friend who trusted me and recommended me for employment where she worked. I was hired as an administrative assistant, and I was also given a position in the after-hours and summer camp programs at the private academy.

The office manager of the school made a job for me, when there seemed to be no job opening. This was clearly a movement of God. She was an encourager to me and became a precious friend while I worked there. Through this work position, I regained some of my lost self-confidence and self-worth. Truly, God's hand was upon me as I performed my duties at the school. He placed me in the exact job I needed, and I exercised abilities with which He had endowed me. Oh, the marvelous wonders of my heavenly Father. I was a diligent employee and prospered in aspects that enabled me to regain dignity. I worked in this capacity for two years before retiring and moving to Fort Worth, Texas, in 2010.

I enjoy precious visits and communications from my children and thirty-three grandchildren and six great grandchildren (at this writing). My heart is full of the joy of the Lord as I serve Him in my church and yield my gifts unto Him. I rejoice as I witness the work of the Lord in my children's lives.

My children are the greatest gifts ever given to me. I cherish them and desire that they rest in God's provision. Our dysfunctional family life during their years at home resulted in a wounding effect on my children's psyche and spiritual wellbeing. Several of the children and I have sought avenues of therapy and deliverance to minister to our broken hearts, minds, and lives. Ultimately, we have acknowledged that God is the supreme Healer. As a parent, one of my most humbling and painful experiences was when God revealed to me some of my failures as a mother. I confessed my failures to Him and asked His forgiveness, and then I asked my children's forgiveness.

Our family's road to recovery following the revelation of our dark cloud of travesty has not been quick or easy but has generated great and marvelous victories when we have yielded ourselves unto Him. Some of my children have come to rest in the saving work of

Jesus. Others have been delivered from drug addictions, and some of us have been liberated from weighty chains including unforgiveness, a judgmental spirit, fear, and the spirit of religion.

I know I have been delivered from the bondage of concealing from others the victories my Savior, my great Warrior has accomplished for me. I had convinced myself, prior to moving to Fort Worth, Texas, that I would just leave the heartbreak and pain of my family's tragedy in Mississippi. It causes me to weep to think that once again I chose *silence* instead of *truth*. Hallelujah! He delivered me.

> *Thou art my hiding place; thou shalt preserve me from trouble; thou shalt compass me about with songs of deliverance (Psalm 32:7 KJV).*

I am now compelled to share these victories, realizing His deliverance of me was not only for me, but for others as well. Consequently, the words that now loom before you in book form are a testimony of my deliverance and are recorded as a tangible comfort, hope, and encouragement for you, my beloved reader. The forces of evil battled me as I opened my mind and spirit to speak *truth* through *my story* to encourage you to not be silent. In the chapter titled "Silence Speaks," the powers of darkness attacked my computer multiple times and kept shutting it down as I labored to expose evil. Truth prevailed. Hallelujah! You too can experience victory and comfort in deliverance.

> *All praise to God, the Father of our Lord Jesus Christ. God is our merciful Father and the source of all comfort. He comforts us in all our troubles so that we can comfort others. When they are troubled, we will be*

> *able to give them the same comfort God has given us (II Corinthians 1:3-4 NLT).*

> *He lifted me out of the pit of despair, out of the mud and the mire. He set my feet on solid ground and steadied me as I walked along. He has given me a new song to sing, a hymn of praise to our God. Many will see what he has done and be amazed. They will put their trust in the Lord (Psalm 40: 2-3 NLT).*

We are commanded to forgive, and by the grace of our loving heavenly Father, to move forward in His plan for our lives. Past experiences and family influence have an impact on all of humankind. Yes, from time-to-time, we have trials or deficits that we can relate to our past or family experiences. We, however, must make a conscious choice not to dwell on past tragedy and know that God does not have plans to harm us.

> *For I know the plans I have for you, says the Lord. They are plans for good and not for disaster, to give you a future and a hope (Jeremiah 29:11 NLT).*

Yes, our Father has a plan for us. He makes known to us an aspect of His plan through His Word that will help us to move forward in victory instead of drowning in past hurts and tragedies. His Word is a powerful provision to comfort us and give us hope.

> *Finally, brethren, whatsoever things are true, whatsoever things are honest, whatsoever things are just, whatsoever things are pure, whatsoever things are lovely, whatsoever things are of good report; if there be any*

virtue, and if there be any praise, think on these things (Philippians 4:8 KJV).

Satan is rampant in the arena of past failures because it is a destructive weapon in his hand to try to defeat the children of God or anyone. If our choice is to *wallow in* or *dwell on* the hurts of the past and engage in the blame game, we will suffer and be defeated. Keeping the pain of past tragedy fresh in our hearts and minds yields depression, overwhelming anguish, and defeat. The past can be beneficial to us used as a teaching source to cause us to seek Him and submit to His way. The only peace that will profit us will flow from the Father and His ways. He is the giver of perfect peace, and this peace will never be found in people, only in Him.

Our God is able to do exceedingly, abundantly above all we ask or think. I have found wonderful freedom in *truth*. What a joy and blessing it is to worship and serve my God daily in liberty. He set this captive free; I had been in bondage to a man and false ideas. Do not make a man or a woman an idol. Do not let people have control of you, only God deserves that power. I discovered this liberty when God became my Deliverer. I had been chained by the idol worship of a man. I had been bound by the teaching that I had to please God through my husband. No person or anything will ever cloud the view of my Savior again.

When Christ died on the cross, our liberty and freedom was secured by His finished work. As we experience deliverance in different areas of our lives, we are living the sweet, yet powerful liberty and freedom He secured for us on Cavalry. This mighty gift of freedom has always existed for us; however, we do not always choose to walk in it. Freedom is the fullness of God working fully in us and through us. The gift of freedom is ours. Do not choose bondage and chains over freedom. The following statement is taken from a series of messages my Pastor delivered in 2016, "Whenever one cannot stop what he is doing, although he does not want to continue to do it, he is experiencing bondage not freedom." Remember His promise to deliver us in Isaiah 61.

> *The Spirit of the Lord God is upon me; because the Lord hath anointed me to preach good tidings unto the meek; he hath sent me to bind up the broken hearted, to proclaim liberty to the captives, and the opening of the prison to them that are bound; To proclaim the acceptable year of the Lord, and the day of vengeance of our God; to comfort all that mourn; To appoint unto them that mourn in Zion, to give unto them beauty for ashes, the oil of joy for mourning, the garment of praise for the spirit of heaviness; that they might be called trees of righteousness, the planting of the Lord, that he might be glorified (Isaiah 61:1-3 KJV).*

Read this scripture again and again as your mind and heart are illuminated and saturated by the power of the blessed Holy Spirit to comprehend the wondrous riches of His gracious provision in His Son, our Savior. May the unveiling of my tattered lace encourage you to not be *silent,* but to speak *truth.* I extol you to look unto Him, our Deliverer and Sustainer. When our pilgrimage journey has finished its course and we are finally home with Him, I like to imagine that we will be blessed to review our glorious battle victories from which we were delivered. You know, the ones when we were certain that we would be swallowed up by our Red Sea, the ones when we thought we would perish in the slime, mud, and mire of our pit of despair, and the ones when we were deluded by the deception of the master liar. Yes, those! Now, our finite minds only see through a glass darkly, but then all things will be crystal clear. I am confident as we rejoice, as the review is presented, we will hear jubilant songs of deliverance during our fiery battles. As phenomenal as the songs and accompanying music will be, nothing will compare to the sound of "...his voice as the sound of many waters..." (Revelation 1:15 KJV) when in the heat of the battle, He commands, *Be Loosed*, and we witness our chains and bonds break. Oh, to view the victory unfold! Nothing man has composed, produced, performed, or fathomed in the world's musical and film economy will compare to the Creator's magnificent deliverance productions. The worldly system would tremble in amazement of the Holy God's productions. "...No eye has seen, no ear has heard, and no mind has imagined what God has prepared for those who love him." (1Corinthians 2:9 NLT)

Freedom is ours; walk in it and rejoice. ***Listen.*** The music of Heaven is playing. Don't you hear the songs of deliverance playing for you?

The End

Made in the USA
Coppell, TX
17 March 2021

51874490R00114